57th Annual Meeting of the Association for Computational Linguistics (ACL 2019)

Tutorial Abstracts

Florence, Italy
28 July – 2 August 2019

ISBN: 978-1-5108-9099-2

Printed from e-media with permission by:

Curran Associates, Inc.
57 Morehouse Lane
Red Hook, NY 12571

Some format issues inherent in the e-media version may also appear in this print version.

Printed by Curran Associates, Inc. (2019)

Association for Computational Linguistics
209 N. Eighth Street
Stroudsburg, Pennsylvania 18360

Phone: 1-570-476-8006
Fax: 1-570-476-0860

acl@aclweb.org

Additional copies of this publication are available from:

Curran Associates, Inc.
57 Morehouse Lane
Red Hook, NY 12571 USA
Phone: 845-758-0400
Fax: 845-758-2633
Email: curran@proceedings.com
Web: www.proceedings.com

ACL 2019

The 57th Annual Meeting
of the Association for Computational Linguistics

Tutorial Abstracts

July 28, 2019
Florence, Italy

Introduction

Welcome to the Tutorials Session of ACL 2019 in Florence, Italy.

The tutorials session at ACL offers attendees the opportunity to learn about new research areas through focused and comprehensive introductions given by expert researchers. The tutorials range from introductory topics of general interest to many areas of our field to specific, cutting-edge topics. It is our hope that these tutorials will be useful to novice researchers and experts alike, and that they will help participants stay informed about the latest developments in our rapidly-growing and rapidly-changing field.

This year, as has been the tradition over the past few years, the tutorials committee included tutorial chairs from three conferences: NAACL-HLT, ACL, and EMNLP-IJCNLP. A total of 46 tutorial proposals were submitted, and these were jointly reviewed by the six tutorial chairs. Nine tutorials were selected for presentation at ACL 2019.

Roughly half of the tutorials selected for ACL this year focus on innovative approaches to modeling language, ranging from deep Bayesian models to unsupervised learning of cross-lingual representations. A second focus area is the computational analysis of discourse, with tutorials on the foundations of discourse analysis as well as interdisciplinary applications of text analysis, from argument mining to analysis of political texts. We hope that this selection of tutorials will be both educational and inspirational.

Many thanks are in order to the people who have made it possible to put together this tutorials session. First, thanks to the ACL general chair Lluís Màrquez and the Web manager Sacha Bourdeaud'Hui. Thanks also to the publication co-chairs Douwe Kiele, Ivan Vulić, Shay Cohen, and Kevin Gimpel. We further thank the local organization co-chairs Alessandro Lenci, Bernardo Magnini, and Simonetta Montemagni, as well as ACL's business manager Priscilla Rasmussen who provided invaluable support – not the least in helping us to accommodate the nine excellent tutorials we selected. Finally, thanks to our co-chairs and co-reviewers Anoop Sarkar and Michael Strube (NAACL-HLT), and also Tim Baldwin and Marine Carpuat (EMNLP-IJCNLP).

We hope you enjoy the tutorials.

ACL 2019 Tutorial Co-chairs
Preslav Nakov
Alexis Palmer

General Chair

Lluís Màrquez, Amazon

Program Chairs

Anna Korhonen, University of Cambridge
David Traum, University of South California

Tutorial Chairs

Preslav Nakov, Qatar Computing Research Institute, HBKU
Alexis Palmer, University of North Texas

Table of Contents

Conference Program

Sunday, July 28, 2019

09:00–12:30 Morning Session

Latent Structure Models for Natural Language Processing
André F. T. Martins, Tsvetomila Mihaylova, Nikita Nangia and Vlad Niculae

Graph-Based Meaning Representations: Design and Processing
Alexander Koller, Stephan Oepen and Weiwei Sun

Discourse Analysis and Its Applications
Shafiq Joty, Giuseppe Carenini, Raymond Ng and Gabriel Murray

Computational Analysis of Political Texts: Bridging Research Efforts Across Communities
Goran Glavaš, Federico Nanni and Simone Paolo Ponzetto

Wikipedia as a Resource for Text Analysis and Retrieval
Marius Pasca

12:30–14:00 Lunch

14:00–17:30 Afternoon Session

Deep Bayesian Natural Language Processing
Jen-Tzung Chien

Unsupervised Cross-Lingual Representation Learning
Sebastian Ruder, Anders Søgaard and Ivan Vulić

Advances in Argument Mining
Katarzyna Budzynska and Chris Reed

Storytelling from Structured Data and Knowledge Graphs : An NLG Perspective
Abhijit Mishra, Anirban Laha, Karthik Sankaranarayanan, Parag Jain and Saravanan Krishnan

Sunday, July 28, 2019 (continued)

Latent Structure Models for Natural Language Processing

André F.T. Martins[ℛ][@] Tsvetomila Mihaylova[ℛ] Nikita Nangia[Υ] and Vlad Niculae[ℛ]
[ℛ]Instituto de Telecomunicações, Lisbon, Portugal
[Υ]Center for Data Science, New York University, US
[@]Unbabel, Lisbon, Portugal
andre.martins@unbabel.com, tsvetomila.mihaylova@gmail.com,
nikitanangia@nyu.edu, vlad@vene.ro

Link to materials:
https://deep-spin.github.io/tutorial/

1 Description

Latent structure models are a powerful tool for modeling compositional data, discovering linguistic structure, and building NLP pipelines (Smith, 2011). Words, sentences, paragraphs, and documents represent the fundamental units in NLP, and their discrete, compositional nature is well suited to combinatorial representations such as trees, sequences, segments, or alignments. When available from human experts, such structured annotations (like syntactic parse trees or part-of-speech information) can help higher-level models perform or generalize better. However, linguistic structure is often **hidden** from practitioners, in which case it becomes useful to model it as a latent variable.

While it is possible to build powerful models that obliviate linguistic structure almost completely (such as LSTMs and Transformer architectures), there are two main reasons why modeling it is desirable: first, incorporating **structural bias** during training can lead to better generalization, since it corresponds to a more informed and more appropriate prior. Second, discovering hidden structure provides better **interpretability**: this is particularly useful when used in conjunction with neural networks, whose typical architectures are not amenable to interpretation. The learnt structure offers highly valuable insight into how the model organizes and composes information.

This tutorial will cover recent advances in latent structure models in NLP. In the last couple of years, the general idea of **hidden linguistic structure** has been married to **latent representation learning** via neural networks. This has allowed powerful modern NLP models to learn to uncover, for example, latent word alignments or parse trees, jointly, in an **unsupervised** or **semi-supervised** fashion, from the signal of higher-level downstream tasks like sentiment analysis or machine translation. This avoids the need for preprocessing data with off-the-shelf tools (e.g., parsers, word aligners) and engineering features based on their outputs; and it is an alternative to techniques based on parameter sharing, transfer learning, multi-task learning, or scaffolding (Swayamdipta et al., 2018; Peters et al., 2018; Devlin et al., 2019; Strubell et al., 2018), as well as techniques that incorporate structural bias directly in model design (Dyer et al., 2016; Shen et al., 2019).

The proposed tutorial is about such **discrete latent structure models**. We discuss their motivation, potential, and limitations, then explore in detail three strategies for designing such models:

- Reinforcement learning;
- Surrogate gradients;
- End-to-end differentiable methods.

A challenge with structured latent models is that they typically involve computing an "argmax" (i.e. finding a best scoring discrete structure such as a parse tree) in the middle of a computation graph. Since this operation has null gradients almost everywhere, gradient backpropagation cannot be used out of the box for training. The methods we cover in this tutorial differ among each other by the way they handle this issue.

Reinforcement learning. In a stochastic computation graph, such methods seek the hidden discrete structures that minimize an expected loss on a downstream task (Yogatama et al., 2017); similar to maximizing an expected reward in reinforcement learning with discrete actions. Estimated stochastic gradients are typically obtained with a combination

Proceedings of the 55th Annual Meeting of the Association for Computational Linguistics, pages 1–5
Vancouver, Canada, July 30 - August 4, 2017.
https://doi.org/10.18653/v1/P17

of Monte Carlo sampling and the score function estimator (a.k.a. REINFORCE, Williams, 1992). Such estimators often suffer from instability and high variance, requiring care (Havrylov et al., 2019).

Surrogate gradients. Such techniques usually involve approximating the gradient of a discrete, argmax-like mapping by the gradient of a continuous relaxation. Examples are the straight-through estimator (Bengio et al., 2013) and the structured projection of intermediate gradients optimization technique (SPIGOT; Peng et al. 2018). In stochastic graphs, surrogate gradients yield biased but lower-variance gradient estimators compared to the score function estimator. Related is the Gumbel softmax (Jang et al., 2017; Maddison et al., 2017; Choi et al., 2018; Maillard and Clark, 2018), which uses the reparametrization trick and a temperature parameter to build a continuous surrogate of the argmax operation, which one can then differentiate over. Structured versions were recently explored by Corro and Titov (2019a,b). One limitation of straight-through estimators is that backpropagating with respect to the sample-independent means may cause discrepancies between the forward and backward pass, which biases learning.

End-to-end differentiable approaches. Here, we directly replace the argmax by a continuous relaxation for which the exact gradient can be computed and backpropagated normally. Examples are structured attention networks and related work (Kim et al., 2017; Maillard et al., 2017; Liu and Lapata, 2018; Mensch and Blondel, 2018), which use marginal inference, or SparseMAP (Niculae et al., 2018a,b), a new inference strategy which yields a sparse set of structures. While the former is usually limited in which the downstream model can only depend on local substructures (not the entire latent structure), the latter allows combining the best of both worlds. Another line of work imbues structure into neural attention via sparsity-inducing priors (Martins and Astudillo, 2016; Niculae and Blondel, 2017; Malaviya et al., 2018).

This tutorial will highlight connections among all these methods, enumerating their strengths and weaknesses. The models we present and analyze have been applied to a wide variety of NLP tasks, including sentiment analysis, natural language inference, language modeling, machine translation, and semantic parsing. In addition, evaluations specific to latent structure recovery have been proposed (Nangia and Bowman, 2018; Williams et al., 2018). Examples and evaluation will be covered throughout the tutorial. After attending the tutorial, a practitioner will be better informed about which method is best suited for their problem.

2 Type of Tutorial & Relationship to Recent Tutorials

The proposed tutorial mixes the **introductory** and **cutting-edge** types. It will offer a gentle introduction to recent advances in structured modeling with **discrete** latent variables, which were not previously covered in any ACL/EMNLP/IJCNLP/NAACL related tutorial.

The closest related topics covered in recent tutorials at NLP conferences are:

- Variational inference and deep generative models (Aziz and Schulz, 2018); [1]
- Deep latent-variable models of natural language (Kim et al., 2018).[2]

Our tutorial offers a complementary perspective in which the latent variables are structured and discrete, corresponding to linguistic structure. We will briefly discuss the modeling alternatives above in the final discussion.

3 Outline

Below we sketch an outline of the tutorial, which will take three hours, separated by a 30-minutes coffee break.

1. Introduction (30 min)
   - Why latent variables?
   - Motivation and examples of latent structure in NLP
   - Continuous vs. discrete latent variables
   - Bypassing latent variables
     - Pipelines / external classifiers
     - Transfer learning / parameter sharing
     - Multi-task learning
   - Challenges: gradients of argmax
   - Categorical versus structured: the simplex and the marginal polytope
2. Reinforcement learning methods (30 min)

[1] https://github.com/philschulz/VITutorial

[2] http://nlp.seas.harvard.edu/latent-nlp-tutorial.html

- SPINN: parsing and classification with shared parameters
- Stochastic computation graphs
- The Score Function Estimator and REINFORCE (application: RL-SPINN with unsupervised parsing)
- Example: the ListOps diagnostic dataset benchmark
- Actor-critic methods & variance reduction

3. Surrogate gradient methods (30 min)
   - Unstructured: straight-through estimators
   - Structured: SPIGOT
   - Sampling categoricals with Gumbel-argmax
   - Gumbel-softmax: reparametrization and straight-through variants
   - Example: Gumbel Tree-LSTM to compose tree structures
   - Perturb-and-MAP / Perturb-and-parse

   Coffee break (30 min)

4. End-to-end differentiable formulations (60 min)
   - Attention mechanisms & hidden alignments
   - Sparse and grouped attention mechanisms
   - Structured attention networks
   - Example: dense / sparse differentiable dynamic programming
   - SparseMAP
   - Relationships with gradient approximation
   - Example: Natural language inference with latent structure (matchings and trees)

5. Closing Remarks and Discussion (30 min)
   - Is it Syntax? Addressing if existing methods learn recognizable grammars
   - Alternative perspectives:
     - Structural bias in model design
     - Deep generative models with continuous latent variables
   - Current open problems and discussion.

4 Breadth

We aim to provide the first unified perspective into multiple related approaches. Of the 31 referenced works, only 6 are co-authored by the presenters. In the outline, the first half presents exclusively work by other researchers and the second half present a mix of our own work and other people's work.

5 Prerequisites and reading

The audience should be comfortable with:

- **math**: basics of differentiability.
- **language**: basic familiarity with the building blocks of structured prediction problems in NLP, e.g., syntax trees and dependency parsing.
- **machine learning**: familiarity with neural networks for NLP, basic understanding of backpropagation and computation graphs.

6 Instructors

André Martins[3] is the Head of Research at Unbabel, a research scientist at Instituto de Telecomunicações, and an invited professor at Instituto Superior Técnico in the University of Lisbon. He received his dual-degree PhD in Language Technologies in 2012 from Carnegie Mellon University and Instituto Superior Técnico. His research interests include natural language processing, machine learning, deep learning, and optimization. He received a best paper award at the Annual Meeting of the Association for Computational Linguistics (ACL) for his work in natural language syntax, and a SCS Honorable Mention at CMU for his PhD dissertation. He is one of the co-founders and organizers of the Lisbon Machine Learning Summer School (LxMLS). He co-presented tutorials at NAACL in 2012, EACL in 2014, and EMNLP in 2014. He co-organized the NAACL 2019 Workshop on Structured Prediction for NLP (http://structuredprediction.github.io/SPNLP19) and the ICLR 2019 Workshop "Deep Reinforcement Learning Meets Structured Prediction".

Tsvetomila Mihaylova[4] is a PhD student in the DeepSPIN project at Instituto de Telecomunicações in Lisbon, Portugal, supervised by André Martins. She is working on empowering neural networks with a planning mechanism for structural search. She has a master's degree in Information Retrieval from the Sofia University, where she was also a teaching assistant in Artificial Intelligence. She is part of the organizers of a shared task in SemEval 2019.

[3] https://andre-martins.github.io
[4] https://tsvm.github.io

Nikita Nangia[5] is a PhD student at New York University, advised by Samuel Bowman. She is working on building neural network systems in NLP that simultaneously do structured prediction and representation learning. This work focuses on finding structure in language without direct supervision and using it for semantic tasks like natural language inference and summarization.

Vlad Niculae[6] is a postdoc in the DeepSPIN project at the Instituto de Telecomunicações in Lisbon, Portugal. His research aims to bring structure and sparsity to neural network hidden layers and latent variables, using ideas from convex optimization, and motivations from natural language processing. He earned a PhD in Computer Science from Cornell University in 2018. He received the inaugural Cornell CS Doctoral Dissertation Award, and co-organized the NAACL 2019 Workshop on Structured Prediction for NLP (`http://structuredprediction.github.io/SPNLP19`).

References

Wilker Aziz and Philip Schulz. 2018. Variational inference and deep generative models. In *Proc. ACL Tutorial Abstracts*.

Yoshua Bengio, Nicholas Léonard, and Aaron Courville. 2013. Estimating or propagating gradients through stochastic neurons for conditional computation. *preprint arXiv:1308.3432*.

Jihun Choi, Kang Min Yoo, and Sang-goo Lee. 2018. Learning to compose task-specific tree structures. In *Proc. AAAI*.

Caio Corro and Ivan Titov. 2019a. Differentiable Perturb-and-Parse: Semi-supervised parsing with a structured variational autoencoder. In *Proc. ICLR*.

Caio Corro and Ivan Titov. 2019b. Learning latent trees with stochastic perturbations and differentiable dynamic programming. In *Proc. ACL*.

Jacob Devlin, Ming-Wei Chang, Kenton Lee, and Kristina Toutanova. 2019. BERT: Pre-training of deep bidirectional transformers for language understanding. In *Proc. NAACL-HLT*.

Chris Dyer, Adhiguna Kuncoro, Miguel Ballesteros, and Noah A Smith. 2016. Recurrent neural network grammars. In *Proc. NAACL-HLT*.

Serhii Havrylov, Germán Kruszewski, and Armand Joulin. 2019. Cooperative learning of disjoint syntax and semantics. In *Proc. NAACL-HLT*.

[5] `https://woollysocks.github.io`

[6] `https://vene.ro`

Eric Jang, Shixiang Gu, and Ben Poole. 2017. Categorical reparametrization with Gumbel-Softmax. In *Proc. ICLR*.

Yoon Kim, Carl Denton, Loung Hoang, and Alexander M Rush. 2017. Structured attention networks. In *Proc. ICLR*.

Yoon Kim, Sam Wiseman, and Alexander Rush. 2018. Deep latent variable models of natural language. In *Proc. EMNLP Tutorial Abstracts*.

Yang Liu and Mirella Lapata. 2018. Learning structured text representations. *TACL*, 6:63–75.

Chris J Maddison, Andriy Mnih, and Yee Whye Teh. 2017. The concrete distribution: A continuous relaxation of discrete random variables. In *Proc. ICLR*.

Jean Maillard and Stephen Clark. 2018. Latent Tree Learning with Differentiable Parsers:Shift-Reduce Parsing and Chart Parsing. In *Proc. ACL*.

Jean Maillard, Stephen Clark, and Dani Yogatama. 2017. Jointly learning sentence embeddings and syntax with unsupervised tree-LSTMs. *preprint arXiv:1705.09189*.

Chaitanya Malaviya, Pedro Ferreira, and André FT Martins. 2018. Sparse and constrained attention for neural machine translation. In *Proc. ACL*.

André FT Martins and Ramón Fernandez Astudillo. 2016. From softmax to sparsemax: A sparse model of attention and multi-label classification. In *Proc. ICML*.

Arthur Mensch and Mathieu Blondel. 2018. Differentiable dynamic programming for structured prediction and attention. In *Proc. ICML*.

Nikita Nangia and Samuel Bowman. 2018. ListOps: A diagnostic dataset for latent tree learning. In *Proc. NAACL Student Research Workshop*.

Vlad Niculae and Mathieu Blondel. 2017. A regularized framework for sparse and structured neural attention. In *Proc. NeurIPS*.

Vlad Niculae, André FT Martins, Mathieu Blondel, and Claire Cardie. 2018a. SparseMAP: Differentiable sparse structured inference. In *Proc. ICML*.

Vlad Niculae, André FT Martins, and Claire Cardie. 2018b. Towards dynamic computation graphs via sparse latent structure. In *Proc. EMNLP*.

Hao Peng, Sam Thomson, and Noah A Smith. 2018. Backpropagating through structured argmax using a SPIGOT. In *Proc. ACL*.

Matthew Peters, Mark Neumann, Mohit Iyyer, Matt Gardner, Christopher Clark, Kenton Lee, and Luke Zettlemoyer. 2018. Deep contextualized word representations. In *Proc. NAACL-HLT*.

Yikang Shen, Tan Shawn, Alessandro Sordoni, and Aaron Courville. 2019. Ordered neurons: Integrating tree structures into recurrent neural networks. In *Proc. ICLR*.

Noah A Smith. 2011. *Linguistic Structure Prediction*. Synth. Lect. Human Lang. Technol. Morgan & Claypool.

Emma Strubell, Patrick Verga, Daniel Andor, David Weiss, and Andrew McCallum. 2018. Linguistically-informed self-attention for semantic role labeling. In *Proc. EMNLP*.

Swabha Swayamdipta, Sam Thomson, Kenton Lee, Luke Zettlemoyer, Chris Dyer, and Noah A Smith. 2018. Syntactic scaffolds for semantic structures. In *Proc. EMNLP*.

Adina Williams, Andrew Drozdov, and Samuel R Bowman. 2018. Do latent tree learning models identify meaningful structure in sentences? *TACL*, 6:253–267.

Ronald J Williams. 1992. Simple statistical gradient-following algorithms for connectionist reinforcement learning. *Machine Learning*, 8(3-4):229–256.

Dani Yogatama, Phil Blunsom, Chris Dyer, Edward Grefenstette, and Wang Ling. 2017. Learning to compose words into sentences with reinforcement learning. In *Proc. ICLR*.

Tutorial at ACL 2019

Graph-Based Meaning Representations: Design and Processing

https://github.com/cfmrp/tutorial

Alexander Koller
Saarland University
koller@coli.uni-saarland.de

Stephan Oepen
University of Oslo
oe@ifi.uio.no

Weiwei Sun
Peking University
ws@pku.edu.cn

Abstract

This tutorial is on representing and processing *sentence meaning* in the form of *labeled directed graphs*. The tutorial will (a) briefly review relevant background in formal and linguistic semantics; (b) semi-formally define a unified abstract view on different flavors of semantic graphs and associated terminology; (c) survey common frameworks for graph-based meaning representation and available graph banks; and (d) offer a technical overview of a representative selection of different parsing approaches.

1 Tutorial Content and Relevance

All things semantic are receiving heightened attention in recent years. Despite remarkable advances in vector-based (continuous, dense, and distributed) encodings of meaning, 'classic' (hierarchically structured and discrete) semantic representations will continue to play an important role in 'making sense' of natural language. While parsing has long been dominated by tree-structured target representations, there is now growing interest in *general graphs* as more expressive and arguably more adequate target structures for sentence-level grammatical analysis beyond surface syntax and in particular for the representation of semantic structure.

Today, the landscape of meaning representation approaches, annotated graph banks, and parsing techniques into these structures is complex and diverse. Graph-based semantic parsing has been a task in almost every Semantic Evaluation (SemEval) exercise since 2014. These shared tasks were based on a variety of different corpora with graph-based meaning annotations (*graph banks*), which differ both in their formal properties and in the facets of meaning they aim to represent. The *relevance* of this tutorial is to clarify this landscape for our research community by providing a unifying view on these graph banks and their associated parsing problems, while working out similarities and differences between common frameworks and techniques.

Based on common-sense linguistic and formal dimensions established in its first part, the tutorial will provide a *coherent, systematized overview* of this field. Participants will be enabled to identify genuine content differences between frameworks as well as to tease apart more superficial variation, for example in terminology or packaging. Furthermore, major current processing techniques for semantic graphs will be reviewed against a *high-level inventory of families of approaches*. This part of the tutorial will emphasize reflections on co-dependencies with specific graph flavors or frameworks, on worst-case and typical time and space complexity, as well as on what guarantees (if any) are obtained on the wellformedness and correctness of output structures.

Kate and Wong (2010) suggest a definition of *semantic parsing* as "the task of mapping natural language sentences into complete formal meaning representations which a computer can execute for some domain-specific application." This view brings along a tacit expectation to map (more or less) directly from a linguistic surface form to an actionable encoding of its intended meaning, e.g. in a database query or even programming language. In this tutorial, we embrace a broader perspective on semantic parsing as it has come to be viewed commonly in recent years. We will review graph-based meaning representations that aim to be *application- and domain-independent*, i.e. seek to provide a reusable intermediate layer of interpretation that captures, in suitably abstract form, relevant constraints that the linguistic signal imposes on interpretation.

Proceedings of the 55th Annual Meeting of the Association for Computational Linguistics, pages 6–11
Vancouver, Canada, July 30 - August 4, 2017.
https://doi.org/10.18653/v1/P17

Tutorial slides and additional materials are available at the following address:

`https://github.com/cfmrp/tutorial`

2 Semantic Graph Banks

In the first part of the tutorial, we will give a systematic overview of the available semantic graph banks. On the one hand, we will distinguish graph banks with respect to the facets of natural language meaning they aim to represent. For instance, some graph banks focus on predicate–argument structure, perhaps with some extensions for polarity or tense, whereas others capture (some) scopal phenomena. Furthermore, while the graphs in most graph banks do not have a precisely defined model theory in the sense of classical linguistic semantics, there are still underlying intuitions about what the nodes of the graphs mean (individual entities and eventualities in the world vs. more abstract objects to which statements about scope and presupposition can attach). We will discuss the different intuitions that underly different graph banks.

On the other hand, we will follow Kuhlmann and Oepen (2016) in classifying graph banks with respect to the relationship they assume between the tokens of the sentence and the nodes of the graph (called *anchoring* of graph fragments onto input sub-strings). We will distinguish three *flavors* of semantic graphs, which by degree of anchoring we will call type (0) to type (2). While we use 'flavor' to refer to formally defined sub-classes of semantic graphs, we will reserve the term 'framework' for a specific linguistic approach to graph-based meaning representation (typically cast in a particular graph flavor, of course).

Type (0) The strongest form of anchoring is obtained in *bi-lexical dependency graphs*, where graph nodes injectively correspond to surface lexical units (tokens). In such graphs, each node is directly linked to a specific token (conversely, there may be semantically empty tokens), and the nodes inherit the linear order of their corresponding tokens. This flavor of semantic graphs was popularized in part through a series of Semantic Dependency Parsing (SDP) tasks at the SemEval exercises in 2014–16 (Oepen et al., 2014, 2015; Che et al., 2016). Prominent linguistic frameworks instantiating this graph flavor include CCG word–word dependencies (CCD; Hockenmaier and Steedman, 2007), Enju Predicate–Argument Structures (PAS; Miyao and Tsujii, 2008), DELPH-IN MRS Bi-Lexical Dependencies (DM; Ivanova et al., 2012) and Prague Semantic Dependencies (PSD; a simplification of the tectogrammatical structures of Hajič et al., 2012).

Type (1) A more general form of *anchored semantic graphs* is characterized by relaxing the correspondence relations between nodes and tokens, while still explicitly annotating the correspondence between nodes and parts of the sentence. Some graph banks of this flavor align nodes with arbitrary parts of the sentence, including subtoken or multi-token sequences, which affords more flexibility in the representation of meaning contributed by, for example, (derivational) affixes or phrasal constructions. Some further allow multiple nodes to correspond to overlapping spans, enabling lexical decomposition (e.g. of causatives or comparatives). Frameworks instantiating this flavor of semantic graphs include Universal Conceptual Cognitive Annotation (UCCA; Abend and Rappoport, 2013; featured in a SemEval 2019 task) and two variants of 'reducing' the underspecified logical forms of Flickinger (2000) and Copestake et al. (2005) into directed graphs, viz. Elementary Dependency Structures (EDS; Oepen and Lønning, 2006) and Dependency Minimal Recursion Semantics (DMRS; Copestake, 2009). All three frameworks serve as target representations in recent parsing research (e.g. Buys and Blunsom, 2017; Chen et al., 2018; Hershcovich et al., 2018).

Type (2) Finally, our framework review will include Abstract Meaning Representation (AMR; Banarescu et al., 2013), which in our hierarchy of graph flavors is considered *unanchored*, in that the correspondence between nodes and tokens is not explicitly annotated. The AMR framework deliberately backgrounds notions of compositionality and derivation. At the same time, AMR frequently invokes lexical decomposition and represents some implicitly expressed elements of meaning, such that AMR graphs quite generally appear to 'abstract' furthest from the surface signal. Since the first general release of an AMR graph bank in 2014, the framework has provided a popular target for semantic parsing and has been the subject of two consecutive tasks at SemEval 2016 and 2017 (May, 2016; May and Priyadarshi, 2017).

3 Processing Semantic Graphs

The creation of large-scale, high-quality semantic graph banks has driven research on *semantic parsing*, where a system is trained to map from natural-language sentences to graphs. There is now a dizzying array of different semantic parsing algorithms, and it is a challenge to keep track of their respective strengths and weaknesses. Different parsing approaches are, of course, more or less effective for graph banks of different flavors (and, at times, even specific frameworks). We will discuss these interactions in the tutorial and organize the research landscape on graph-based semantic parsing along three dimensions.

Decoding strategy Semantic parsers differ with respect to the type of algorithm that is used to compute the graph. These include factorization-based methods, which factorize the score of a graph into parts for smaller substrings and can then apply dynamic programming to search for the best graph, as well as transition-based methods, which learn to make individual parsing decisions for each token in the sentence. Some neural techniques also make use of an encoder-decoder architecture, as in neural machine translation.

Compositionality Semantic parsers also differ with respect to whether they assume that the graph-based semantic representations are constructed compositionally. Some approaches follow standard linguistic practice in assuming that the graphs have a latent compositional structure and try to reconstruct it explicitly or implicitly during parsing. Others are more agnostic and simply predict the edges of the target graph without regard to such linguistic assumptions.

Structural information Finally, semantic parsers differ with respect to how structure information is represented. Some model the target graph directly, whereas others use probability models that score a tree which evaluates to the target graph (e.g. a syntactic derivation tree or a term over a graph algebra). This choice interacts with the compositionality dimension, in that tree-based models for graph parsing go together well with compositional models.

4 Tutorial Structure

We have organized the content of the tutorial into the following blocks, which add up to a total of three hours of presentation. The references below are illustrative of the content in each block; in the tutorial itself, we will present one or two approaches per block in detail while treating others more superficially.

(1) Linguistic Foundations: Layers of Sentence Meaning

(2) Formal Foundations: Labeled Directed Graphs

(3) Meaning Representation Frameworks and Graph Banks

- Bi-Lexical semantic dependencies (Hockenmaier and Steedman, 2007; Miyao and Tsujii, 2008; Hajič et al., 2012; **Ivanova et al., 2012**; Che et al., 2016);
- Universal Conceptual Cognitive Annotation (UCCA; **Abend and Rappoport, 2013**);
- Graph-Based Minimal Recursion Semantics (EDS and DMRS; **Oepen and Lønning, 2006**; Copestake, 2009);
- Abstract Meaning Representation (AMR; **Banarescu et al., 2013**);
- Non-Graph Representations: Discourse Representation Structures (DRS; Basile et al., 2012);
- Contrastive review of selected examples across frameworks;
- Availability of training and evaluation data; shared tasks; state-of-the-art empirical results.

(4) Parsing into Semantic Graphs

- Parser evaluation: quantifying semantic graph similarity;
- Parsing sub-tasks: segmentation, concept identification, relation detection, structural validation;
- Composition-based methods (Callmeier, 2000; Bos et al., 2004; Artzi et al., 2015; **Groschwitz et al., 2018**; Lindemann et al., 2019; **Chen et al., 2018**);
- Factorization-based methods (**Flanigan et al., 2014**; Kuhlmann and Jonsson, 2015; Peng et al., 2017; **Dozat and Manning, 2018**);

- Transition-based methods (Sagae and Tsujii, 2008; Wang et al., 2015; Buys and Blunsom, 2017; Hershcovich et al., 2017);
- Translation-based methods (Konstas et al., 2017; Peng et al., 2018; Stanovsky and Dagan, 2018);
- Cross-framework parsing and multi-task learning (Peng et al., 2017; Hershcovich et al., 2018; Stanovsky and Dagan, 2018);
- Cross-lingual parsing methods (Evang and Bos, 2016; Damonte and Cohen, 2018; Zhang et al., 2018);
- Contrastive discussion across frameworks, approaches, and languages.

(5) Outlook: Applications of Semantic Graphs

5 Content Breadth

Each of us has contributed research to the design of meaning representation frameworks, creation of semantic graph banks, and and/or the development of meaning representation parsing systems. Nonetheless, both the design and the processing of graph banks are highly active research areas, and our own work will not represent more than a fifth of the total tutorial content.

6 Participant Background

An understanding of basic parsing techniques (chart-based and transition-based) and a familiarity with basic neural techniques (feed-forward and recurrent networks, encoder–decoder) will be useful.

7 Presenters

The tutorial will be presented jointly by three experts with partly overlapping and partly complementary expertise. Each will contribute about one third of the content, and each will be involved in multiple parts of the tutorial.

Alexander Koller
Department of Language Science and Technology, Saarland University, Germany
koller@coli.uni-saarland.de
http://www.coli.uni-saarland.de/~koller

Alexander Koller received his PhD in 2004, with a thesis on underspecified processing of semantic ambiguities using graph-based representations. His research interests span a variety of topics including parsing, generation, the expressive capacity of representation formalisms for natural language, and semantics. Within semantics, he has published extensively on semantic parsing using both grammar-based and neural approaches. His most recent work in this field (Groschwitz et al., 2018) achieved state-of-the-art semantic parsing accuracy for AMR using neural supertagging and dependency in the context of a compositional model.

Stephan Oepen
Department of Informatics, University of Oslo, Norway
oe@ifi.uio.no
https://www.mn.uio.no/ifi/english/people/aca/oe/

Stephan Oepen studied Linguistics, German and Russian Philology, Computer Science, and Computational Linguistics at Berlin, Volgograd, and Saarbrücken. He has worked extensively on constraint-based parsing and realization, on the design of broad-coverage meaning representations and the syntax–semantics interface, and on the use of syntactico-semantic structure in natural language understanding applications. He has been a co-developer of the LinGO English Resource Grammar (ERG) since the mid-1990s, has helped create the Redwoods Treebank of scope-underspecified MRS meaning representations, and has chaired two SemEval tasks on Semantic Dependency Parsing as well as the First Shared Task on Cross-Framework Meaning Representation Parsing (MRP) at the 2019 Conference for Computational Language Learning.

Weiwei Sun
Institute of Computer Science and Technology, Peking University, China
ws@pku.edu.cn
https://wsun106.github.io/

Weiwei Sun completed her Ph.D. in the Department of Computational Linguistics from Saarland University under the supervision of Prof. Hans Uszkoreit. Before that, she studied at Peking University, where she obtained BA in Linguistics, and BS and MS in Computer Science. Her research lies at the intersection of computational linguistics and natural language processing. The main topic is symbolic and statistical parsing, with a special focus on parsing into semantic graphs of various flavors. She has repeatedly chaired teams that have submitted top-performing systems to recent SemEval shared tasks and has continuously advanced both the state of the art in semantic parsing in terms of empirical results and the understanding of how design decisions in different schools of linguistic graph representations impact formal and algorithmic complexity.

References

Omri Abend and Ari Rappoport. 2013. Universal Conceptual Cognitive Annotation (UCCA). In *Proceedings of the 51th Meeting of the Association for Computational Linguistics*, pages 228–238, Sofia, Bulgaria.

Yoav Artzi, Kenton Lee, and Luke Zettlemoyer. 2015. Broad-coverage CCG semantic parsing with AMR. In *Proceedings of the 2015 Conference on Empirical Methods in Natural Language Processing*, pages 1699–1710, Lisbon, Portugal.

Laura Banarescu, Claire Bonial, Shu Cai, Madalina Georgescu, Kira Griffitt, Ulf Hermjakob, Kevin Knight, Philipp Koehn, Martha Palmer, and Nathan Schneider. 2013. Abstract Meaning Representation for sembanking. In *Proceedings of the 7th Linguistic Annotation Workshop and Interoperability with Discourse*, pages 178–186, Sofia, Bulgaria.

Valerio Basile, Johan Bos, Kilian Evang, and Noortje Venhuizen. 2012. Developing a large semantically annotated corpus. In *Proceedings of the 8th International Conference on Language Resources and Evaluation*, pages 3196–3200, Istanbul, Turkey.

Johan Bos, Stephen Clark, Mark Steedman, James R. Curran, and Julia Hockenmaier. 2004. Wide-coverage semantic representations from a CCG parser. In *Proceedings of the 20th International Conference on Computational Linguistics*, pages 1240–1246, Geneva, Switzerland.

Jan Buys and Phil Blunsom. 2017. Robust incremental neural semantic graph parsing. In *Proceedings of the 55th Meeting of the Association for Computational Linguistics*, pages 158–167, Vancouver, Canada.

Ulrich Callmeier. 2000. PET. A platform for experimentation with efficient HPSG processing techniques. *Natural Language Engineering*, 6(1):99–108.

Wanxiang Che, Yanqiu Shao, Ting Liu, and Yu Ding. 2016. SemEval-2016 task 9: Chinese semantic dependency parsing. In *Proceedings of the 10th International Workshop on Semantic Evaluation*, pages 1074–1080, San Diego, CA, USA.

Yufei Chen, Weiwei Sun, and Xiaojun Wan. 2018. Accurate SHRG-based semantic parsing. In *Proceedings of the 56th Meeting of the Association for Computational Linguistics*, pages 408–418, Melbourne, Australia.

Ann Copestake. 2009. Slacker semantics. Why superficiality, dependency and avoidance of commitment can be the right way to go. In *Proceedings of the 12th Meeting of the European Chapter of the Association for Computational Linguistics*, pages 1–9, Athens, Greece.

Ann Copestake, Dan Flickinger, Carl Pollard, and Ivan A. Sag. 2005. Minimal Recursion Semantics. An introduction. *Research on Language and Computation*, 3(4):281–332.

Marco Damonte and Shay B. Cohen. 2018. Cross-lingual Abstract Meaning Representation parsing. In *Proceedings of the 2015 Conference of the North American Chapter of the Association for Computational Linguistics*, pages 1146–1155, New Orleans, LA, USA.

Timothy Dozat and Christopher D. Manning. 2018. Simpler but more accurate semantic dependency parsing. In *Proceedings of the 56th Meeting of the Association for Computational Linguistics*, pages 484–490, Melbourne, Australia.

Kilian Evang and Johan Bos. 2016. Cross-lingual learning of an open-domain semantic parser. In *Proceedings of the 26th International Conference on Computational Linguistics*, pages 579–588, Osaka, Japan.

Jeffrey Flanigan, Sam Thomson, Jaime Carbonell, Chris Dyer, and Noah A. Smith. 2014. A discriminative graph-based parser for the Abstract Meaning Representation. In *Proceedings of the 52nd Meeting of the Association for Computational Linguistics*, pages 1426–1436, Baltimore, MD, USA.

Dan Flickinger. 2000. On building a more efficient grammar by exploiting types. *Natural Language Engineering*, 6 (1):15–28.

Jonas Groschwitz, Matthias Lindemann, Meaghan Fowlie, Mark Johnson, and Alexander Koller. 2018. AMR dependency parsing with a typed semantic algebra. In *Proceedings of the 56th Meeting of the Association for Computational Linguistics*, pages 1831–1841, Melbourne, Australia.

Jan Hajič, Eva Hajičová, Jarmila Panevová, Petr Sgall, Ondřej Bojar, Silvie Cinková, Eva Fučíková, Marie Mikulová, Petr Pajas, Jan Popelka, Jiří Semecký, Jana Šindlerová, Jan Štěpánek, Josef Toman, Zdeňka Urešová, and Zdeněk Žabokrtský. 2012. Announcing Prague Czech-English Dependency Treebank 2.0. In *Proceedings of the 8th International Conference on Language Resources and Evaluation*, pages 3153–3160, Istanbul, Turkey.

Daniel Hershcovich, Omri Abend, and Ari Rappoport. 2017. A transition-based directed acyclic graph parser for UCCA. In *Proceedings of the 55th Meeting of the Association for Computational Linguistics*, pages 1127–1138, Vancouver, Canada.

Daniel Hershcovich, Omri Abend, and Ari Rappoport. 2018. Multitask parsing across semantic representations. In *Proceedings of the 56th Meeting of the Association for Computational Linguistics*, pages 373–385, Melbourne, Australia.

Julia Hockenmaier and Mark Steedman. 2007. CCGbank. A corpus of CCG derivations and dependency structures extracted from the Penn Treebank. *Computational Linguistics*, 33:355–396.

Angelina Ivanova, Stephan Oepen, Lilja Øvrelid, and Dan Flickinger. 2012. Who did what to whom? A contrastive study of syntacto-semantic dependencies. In *Proceedings of the 6th Linguistic Annotation Workshop*, pages 2–11, Jeju, Republic of Korea.

Rohit J. Kate and Yuk Wah Wong. 2010. Semantic parsing. The task, the state of the art and the future. In *Tutorial Abstracts of the 20th Meeting of the Association for Computational Linguistics*, page 6, Uppsala, Sweden.

Ioannis Konstas, Srinivasan Iyer, Mark Yatskar, Yejin Choi, and Luke Zettlemoyer. 2017. Neural AMR. Sequence-to-sequence models for parsing and generation. In *Proceedings of the 55th Meeting of the Association for Computational Linguistics*, pages 146–157, Vancouver, Canada.

Marco Kuhlmann and Peter Jonsson. 2015. Parsing to noncrossing dependency graphs. *Transactions of the Association for Computational Linguistics*, 3:559–570.

Marco Kuhlmann and Stephan Oepen. 2016. Towards a catalogue of linguistic graph banks. *Computational Linguistics*, 42(4):819–827.

Matthias Lindemann, Jonas Groschwitz, and Alexander Koller. 2019. Compositional semantic parsing across graphbanks. In *Proceedings of ACL (Short Papers)*, Florence, Italy.

Jonathan May. 2016. SemEval-2016 Task 8. Meaning representation parsing. In *Proceedings of the 10th International Workshop on Semantic Evaluation*, pages 1063–1073, San Diego, CA, USA.

Jonathan May and Jay Priyadarshi. 2017. SemEval-2017 Task 9. Abstract Meaning Representation parsing and generation. In *Proceedings of the 11th International Workshop on Semantic Evaluation*, pages 536–545.

Yusuke Miyao and Jun'ichi Tsujii. 2008. Feature forest models for probabilistic HPSG parsing. *Computational Linguistics*, 34(1):35–80.

John Nerbonne. 1994. Book review. Computational linguistics and formal semantics. *Computational Linguistics*, 20(1):131–136.

Stephan Oepen, Marco Kuhlmann, Yusuke Miyao, Daniel Zeman, Silvie Cinková, Dan Flickinger, Jan Hajič, and Zdeňka Urešová. 2015. SemEval 2015 Task 18. Broad-coverage semantic dependency parsing. In *Proceedings of the 9th International Workshop on Semantic Evaluation*, pages 915–926, Denver, CO, USA.

Stephan Oepen, Marco Kuhlmann, Yusuke Miyao, Daniel Zeman, Dan Flickinger, Jan Hajič, Angelina Ivanova, and Yi Zhang. 2014. SemEval 2014 Task 8. Broad-coverage semantic dependency parsing. In *Proceedings of the 8th International Workshop on Semantic Evaluation*, pages 63–72, Dublin, Ireland.

Stephan Oepen and Jan Tore Lønning. 2006. Discriminant-based MRS banking. In *Proceedings of the 5th International Conference on Language Resources and Evaluation*, pages 1250–1255, Genoa, Italy.

Hao Peng, Sam Thomson, and Noah A. Smith. 2017. Deep multitask learning for semantic dependency parsing. In *Proceedings of the 55th Meeting of the Association for Computational Linguistics*, pages 2037–2048, Vancouver, Canada.

Xiaochang Peng, Linfeng Song, Daniel Gildea, and Giorgio Satta. 2018. Sequence-to-sequence models for cache transition systems. In *Proceedings of the 56th Meeting of the Association for Computational Linguistics*, pages 1842–1852, Melbourne, Australia.

Kenji Sagae and Jun'ichi Tsujii. 2008. Shift-reduce dependency DAG parsing. In *Proceedings of the 22nd International Conference on Computational Linguistics*, pages 753–760, Manchester, UK.

Gabriel Stanovsky and Ido Dagan. 2018. Semantics as a foreign language. In *Proceedings of the 2018 Conference on Empirical Methods in Natural Language Processing*, pages 2412–2421, Brussels, Belgium.

Chuan Wang, Nianwen Xue, and Sameer Pradhan. 2015. A transition-based algorithm for AMR parsing. In *Proceedings of the 2015 Conference of the North American Chapter of the Association for Computational Linguistics*, pages 366–375, Denver, CO, USA.

Sheng Zhang, Xutai Ma, Rachel Rudinger, Kevin Duh, and Benjamin Van Durme. 2018. Cross-lingual decompositional semantic parsing. In *Proceedings of the 2018 Conference on Empirical Methods in Natural Language Processing*, pages 1664–1675, Brussels, Belgium.

Discourse Analysis and Its Applications

Shafiq Joty*, **Giuseppe Carenini**†, **Raymond T. Ng**†, **and Gabriel Murray**§
*Nanyang Technological University, Salesforce Research Asia, Singapore
†University of British Columbia, Vancouver, Canada
§University of the Fraser Valley, Abbotsford, Canada
*srjoty@ntu.edu.sg, §gabriel.murray@ufv.ca
†{carenini,rng}@cs.ubc.ca

Abstract

Discourse processing is a suite of Natural Language Processing (NLP) tasks to uncover linguistic structures from texts at several levels, which can support many downstream applications. This involves identifying the topic structure, the coherence structure, the coreference structure, and the conversation structure for conversational discourse. Taken together, these structures can inform text summarization, machine translation, essay scoring, sentiment analysis, information extraction, question answering, and thread recovery. The tutorial starts with an overview of basic concepts in discourse analysis – monologue vs. conversation, synchronous vs. asynchronous conversation, and key linguistic structures in discourse analysis. We also give an overview of linguistic structures and corresponding discourse analysis tasks that discourse researchers are generally interested in, as well as key applications on which these discourse structures have an impact.

1 Motivation

Discourse analysis has been a fundamental problem in the ACL community, where the focus is to develop tools to automatically model language phenomena that go beyond the individual sentences. With the ongoing neural revolution, as the methods become more effective and flexible, analysis and interpretability beyond the sentence-level is of particular interests for many core language processing tasks like language modeling (Ji et al., 2016) and applications such as machine translation and its evaluation (Sennrich, 2018; Läubli et al., 2018; Joty et al., 2017), text categorization (Ji and Smith, 2017), and sentiment analysis (Nejat et al., 2017). With the advent of Internet technologies, new forms of discourse are emerging (e.g., emails and discussion forums) with novel set of challenges for the computational models. Furthermore, most computational models for discourse analysis are also going through a paradigm shift from traditional statistical models to deep neural models. Considering all these novel aspects at once, this tutorial is quite timely for the community, by providing the attendees with an up-to-date, critical overview of existing approaches and their evaluations, applications, and future challenges.

2 Tutorial Outline

We start with an overview of basic concepts in discourse analysis – monologue vs. conversation, synchronous vs. asynchronous conversation, and key linguistic structures in discourse analysis. Attendees then get to learn about coherence structure and discourse parsers. We give a critical overview of different discourse theories, and available datasets annotated according to these formalisms. We cover methods for RST- and PDTB-style discourse parsing. We cover traditional methods along with the most recent works using deep neural networks, interpret them and compare their performances on benchmark datasets.

Next, we discuss coherence models to evaluate monologues and conversations based on their coherence. We then show applications (evaluation tasks) of coherence models and discourse parsers. Special attention is paid to the new emerging applications of discourse analysis such as machine translation and its evaluation, sentiment analysis, and abstractive summarization.

In the final part of the tutorial, we cover conversational structures (*e.g.,* speech acts, thread structure), computational methods to extract such structures, and their utility in downstream applications (*e.g.,* conversation summarization). Again, evaluation metrics and approaches will be discussed and compared. We conclude with an interactive discussion of future challenges for discourse anal-

Proceedings of the 55th Annual Meeting of the Association for Computational Linguistics, pages 12–17
Vancouver, Canada, July 30 - August 4, 2017. ©2017 Association for Computational Linguistics
https://doi.org/10.18653/v1/P17

ysis and its applications. In the following, we give a detailed breakdown of the tutorial content.

A. Introduction [25 mins]

1. Discourse & its different forms
   (a) Monologue
   (b) Synchronous & asynchronous conversations
   (c) Modalities: written & spoken
2. Two discourse phenomena
   (a) Coherence
   (b) Cohesion
3. Linguistic structures in discourse & discourse analysis tasks
   (a) Coherence structure ⇒ Discourse segmentation & parsing
   (b) Coherence models ⇒ Coherence evaluation
   (c) Topic structure ⇒ Topic segmentation & labeling [not covered in this tutorial]
   (d) Coreference structure ⇒ Coreference resolution [not covered in this tutorial]
   (e) Conversational structure ⇒ Disentanglement & reply-to structure, speech act recognition
4. Applications of discourse analysis

B. Coherence Structure, Corpora & Discourse Parsing [45 mins]

1. Discourse theories & coherence relations
   (a) Rhetorical Structure Theory (RST) & RST Treebank (Carlson et al., 2002) & Instructional domain (Subba and Di Eugenio, 2009)
   (b) Discourse Lexicalized Tree Adjoining Grammar (D-LTAG) & Penn Discourse Treebank (PDTB) (Prasad et al., 2005)
2. Discourse connectives & unsupervised relation identification
   (a) Role of connectives in RST & PDTB
   (b) Identifying discourse connectives
   (c) Implicit and explicit relations
3. Discourse parsing in RST
   (a) The tasks: discourse segmentation and parsing
   (b) Role of syntax
   (c) Traditional models – SPADE (Soricut and Marcu, 2003), HILDA (duVerle and Prendinger, 2009), CODRA (Joty et al., 2015), CRF-based model (Feng and Hirst, 2014).
   (d) Neural models (Ji and Eisenstein, 2014; Li et al., 2014, 2016; Morey et al., 2017)
   (e) State-of-the-Art (Wang et al., 2017; Lin et al., 2019)
   (f) Evaluation & Discussion
4. Discourse parsing in PDTB
   (a) The tasks: relation sense identification and scope disambiguation
   (b) Statistical models (Pitler and Nenkova, 2009; Ziheng et al., 2014)
   (c) Neural models (Ji and Eisenstein, 2015; Lan et al., 2017)
   (d) Evaluation & Discussion
5. Final remarks
   (a) Tree vs. graph structure
   (b) Discourse Graphbank

C. Coffee Break [15 mins]

D. Coherence Models & Applications of Discourse [45 mins]

1. Overview of coherence models
   (a) Entity grid and its extensions (Barzilay and Lapata, 2008; Elsner and Charniak, 2011b; Guinaudeau and Strube, 2013)
   (b) Discourse relation based model (Lin et al., 2011; Pitler and Nenkova, 2008)
   (c) Neural coherence models (Mohiuddin et al., 2018; Li and Jurafsky, 2017; Mesgar and Strube, 2018)
   (d) Coherence models for conversations (Elsner and Charniak, 2011a; Mohiuddin et al., 2018)
2. Evaluation tasks
   (a) Sentence ordering (Discrimination, Insertion)
   (b) Summary coherence rating
   (c) Readability assessment

(d) Chat disentanglement

(e) Thread reconstruction

3. Applications of discourse

   (a) Summarization
   (b) Generation
   (c) Sentiment analysis
   (d) Machine translation

E. Conversational Structure [35 mins]

1. Conversational structures

   (a) Speech (or dialog) acts in synchronous and asynchronous conversations
   (b) Reply-to (thread) structure in asynchronous conversations (Carenini et al., 2007)
   (c) Conversation disentanglement in synchronous conversations

2. Computational models

   (a) Speech act recognition models (Stolcke et al., 2000; Cohen et al., 2004; Ritter et al., 2010; Joty et al., 2011; Paul, 2012; Joty and Hoque, 2016; Mohiuddin et al., 2019)
   (b) Thread reconstruction models (Shen et al., 2006; Wang et al., 2008, 2011a,b)
   (c) Conversation disentanglement models (Elsner and Charniak, 2008, 2011a)

3. Evaluation & Summary of results

F. Future Challenges [15 mins]

1. Learning from limited annotated data

2. Language & domain transfer

3. Discourse generation

4. New emerging applications

Link to the Slides Our tutorial slides will be made available at `https://ntunlpsg.github.io/project/acl19tutorial/`

2.1 Prerequisites

Prior knowledge in basic machine learning, NLP (*e.g.*, parsing methods, machine translation), and deep learning models is essential to understand the content of this tutorial.

2.2 Similar Tutorial

We gave a similar tutorial (shorter version) at the 2018 IEEE International Conference on Data Mining (ICDM-2018), a top conference in data mining. The slides of that tutorial can be found at `https://ntunlpsg.github.io/project/icdmtutorial/`.

3 Instructors

Dr. Shafiq Joty[1] is an Assistant Professor at the School of Computer Science and Engineering, NTU. He is also a senior research manager at the Salesforce AI Research lab. He holds a PhD in Computer Science from the University of British Columbia. His work has primarily focused on developing discourse analysis tools (e.g., discourse parser, coherence model, topic model, dialogue act recognizer), and exploiting these tools effectively in downstream applications like machine translation, summarization, and sentiment analysis. Apart from discourse and its applications, he has also developed novel machine learning models for question answering, machine translation, image/video captioning, visual question answering, and opinion analysis. His work has appeared in major journals and conferences such as CL, JAIR, CSL, ACL, EMNLP, NAACL, IJCAI, CVPR, ECCV, and ICWSM. He served as an area chair for ACL-2019 (QA track) and EMNLP-2019 (Discourse track) and a senior program committee member for IJCAI 2019. Shafiq is a recipient of NSERC CGS-D scholarship and Microsoft Research Excellent Intern award.

Dr. Giuseppe Carenini[2] is a Professor in Computer Science at UBC. Giuseppe has broad interdisciplinary interests. His work on NLP and information visualization to support decision making has been published in over 100 peer-reviewed papers (including best paper at UMAP-14 and ACM-TiiS-14). He was the area chair for ACL'09 "Sentiment Analysis, Opinion Mining, and Text Classification" , NAACL'12 and EMNLP'19 for "Summarization and Generation", ACL'19 for Discourse; the Program Co-Chair for IUI 2015, and the Program Co-Chair for SigDial 2016. He has also co-edited an ACM-TIST Special Issue on "Intelligent Visual Interfaces for Text Analysis". In 2011, he published a co-authored book on "Meth-

[1] https://raihanjoty.github.io/

[2] https://www.cs.ubc.ca/~carenini/

ods for Mining and Summarizing Text Conversations". He has also extensively collaborated with industrial partners, including Microsoft and IBM. He was awarded a Google Research Award, an IBM CASCON Best Exhibit Award, and a Yahoo Faculty Research Award in 2007, 2010 and 2016 respectively.

Dr. Raymond T. Ng[3] is a Professor in Computer Science and the Director of the Data Science Institute at UBC. His main research area for the past two decades is on data mining, with a specific focus on health informatics and text mining. He has published over 180 peer-reviewed publications on data clustering, outlier detection, OLAP processing, health informatics and text mining. He is the recipient of two best paper awards from the 2001 ACM SIGKDD conference, the premier data mining conference in the world, and the 2005 ACM SIGMOD conference, one of the top database conferences worldwide. For the past decade, he has co-led several large-scale genomic projects funded by Genome Canada, Genome BC and industrial collaborators. Since the inception of the PROOF Centre of Excellence, which focuses on biomarker development for end-stage organ failures, he has held the position of the Chief Informatics Officer of the Centre. From 2009 to 2014, he was the associate director of the NSERC-funded strategic network on business intelligence. Since 2016, he has been the holder of the Canadian Research Chair on Data Science and Analytics.

Dr. Gabriel Murray[4] is an Associate Professor in Computer Information Systems at the University of the Fraser Valley (UFV). His background is in computational linguistics and multimodal speech and language processing. He holds a PhD in Informatics from the University of Edinburgh, completed under the supervision of Drs. Steve Renals and Johanna Moore. His research has focused on various aspects of multimodal conversational data, including automatic summarization and sentiment detection for group discussions. Recent research also focuses on predicting group performance and participant affect in conversational data. In 2011, Dr. Murray co-authored the book "Methods for Mining and Summarizing Text Conversations".

[3]https://www.cs.ubc.ca/~rng

[4]https://www.ufv.ca/cis/faculty-and-staff/murray-gabriel.htm

References

Regina Barzilay and Mirella Lapata. 2008. Modeling local coherence: An entity-based approach. *Computational Linguistics*, 34(1):1–34.

G. Carenini, R. T. Ng, and X. Zhou. 2007. Summarizing Email Conversations with Clue Words. In *Proceedings of the 16th international conference on World Wide Web*, WWW'07, pages 91–100, Banff, Canada. ACM.

Lynn Carlson, Daniel Marcu, and Mary Ellen Okurowski. 2002. RST Discourse Treebank (RST–DT) LDC2002T07. *Linguistic Data Consortium, Philadelphia.*

William W. Cohen, Vitor R. Carvalho, and Tom M. Mitchell. 2004. Learning to Classify Email into "Speech Acts". In *Proceedings of the 2004 Conference on Empirical Methods in Natural Language Processing*, EMNLP'04, pages 309–316.

David duVerle and Helmut Prendinger. 2009. A Novel Discourse Parser based on Support Vector Machine Classification. In *Proceedings of the Joint Conference of the 47th Annual Meeting of the ACL and the 4th International Joint Conference on Natural Language Processing of the AFNLP*, pages 665–673, Suntec, Singapore. ACL.

Micha Elsner and Eugene Charniak. 2008. Coreference-inspired coherence modeling. In *Proceedings of the 46th Annual Meeting of the Association for Computational Linguistics on Human Language Technologies: Short Papers*, HLT-Short '08, pages 41–44, Columbus, Ohio. Association for Computational Linguistics.

Micha Elsner and Eugene Charniak. 2011a. Disentangling chat with local coherence models. In *Proceedings of the 49th Annual Meeting of the Association for Computational Linguistics: Human Language Technologies - Volume 1*, HLT '11, pages 1179–1189, Stroudsburg, PA, USA. Association for Computational Linguistics.

Micha Elsner and Eugene Charniak. 2011b. Extending the entity grid with entity-specific features. In *Proceedings of the 49th Annual Meeting of the Association for Computational Linguistics: Human Language Technologies: Short Papers - Volume 2*, HLT '11, pages 125–129, Portland, Oregon. Association for Computational Linguistics.

Vanessa Wei Feng and Graeme Hirst. 2014. A linear-time bottom-up discourse parser with constraints and post-editing. In *Proceedings of the 52nd Annual Meeting of the Association for Computational Linguistics (Volume 1: Long Papers)*, pages 511–521. Association for Computational Linguistics.

Camille Guinaudeau and Michael Strube. 2013. Graph-based local coherence modeling. In *Proceedings of the 51st Annual Meeting of the Association for Computational Linguistics, ACL 2013, 4-9 August 2013, Sofia, Bulgaria, Volume 1: Long Papers*, pages 93–103.

Yangfeng Ji and Jacob Eisenstein. 2014. Representation learning for text-level discourse parsing. In *Proceedings of the 52nd Annual Meeting of the Association for Computational Linguistics (Volume 1: Long Papers)*, pages 13–24, Baltimore, Maryland. ACL.

Yangfeng Ji and Jacob Eisenstein. 2015. One vector is not enough: Entity-augmented distributed semantics for discourse relations. *Transactions of the Association for Computational Linguistics*, 3:329–344.

Yangfeng Ji, Gholamreza Haffari, and Jacob Eisenstein. 2016. A latent variable recurrent neural network for discourse-driven language models. In *Proceedings of the 2016 Conference of the North American Chapter of the Association for Computational Linguistics: Human Language Technologies*, pages 332–342. Association for Computational Linguistics.

Yangfeng Ji and Noah A. Smith. 2017. Neural discourse structure for text categorization. In *Proceedings of the 55th Annual Meeting of the Association for Computational Linguistics (Volume 1: Long Papers)*, pages 996–1005. Association for Computational Linguistics.

Shafiq Joty, Giuseppe Carenini, and Chin-Yew Lin. 2011. Unsupervised Modeling of Dialog Acts in Asynchronous Conversations. In *Proceedings of the twenty second International Joint Conference on Artificial Intelligence*, IJCAI'11, Barcelona, Spain.

Shafiq Joty, Giuseppe Carenini, and Raymond T Ng. 2015. CODRA: A Novel Discriminative Framework for Rhetorical Analysis. *Computational Linguistics*, 41:3:385–435.

Shafiq Joty, Francisco Guzmán, Llus Mrquez, and Preslav Nakov. 2017. Discourse structure in machine translation evaluation. *Computational Linguistics*, 43:4:683–722.

Shafiq Joty and Enamul Hoque. 2016. Speech act modeling of written asynchronous conversations with task-specific embeddings and conditional structured models. In *Proceedings of the 54th Annual Meeting of the Association for Computational Linguistics (Volume 1: Long Papers)*, pages 1746–1756, Berlin, Germany. Association for Computational Linguistics.

Man Lan, Jianxiang Wang, Yuanbin Wu, Zheng-Yu Niu, and Haifeng Wang. 2017. Multi-task attention-based neural networks for implicit discourse relationship representation and identification. In *Proceedings of the 2017 Conference on Empirical Methods in Natural Language Processing*, pages 1299–1308. Association for Computational Linguistics.

Samuel Läubli, Rico Sennrich, and Martin Volk. 2018. Has Machine Translation Achieved Human Parity? A Case for Document-level Evaluation. In *Proceedings of the 2018 Conference on Empirical Methods in Natural Language Processing*, pages 4791–4796. Association for Computational Linguistics.

Jiwei Li and Dan Jurafsky. 2017. Neural net models of open-domain discourse coherence. In *Proceedings of the 2017 Conference on Empirical Methods in Natural Language Processing*, pages 198–209, Copenhagen, Denmark. Association for Computational Linguistics.

Jiwei Li, Rumeng Li, and Eduard Hovy. 2014. Recursive deep models for discourse parsing. In *Proceedings of the 2014 Conference on Empirical Methods in Natural Language Processing (EMNLP)*, pages 2061–2069, Doha, Qatar. ACL.

Qi Li, Tianshi Li, and Baobao Chang. 2016. Discourse parsing with attention-based hierarchical neural networks. In *Proceedings of the 2016 Conference on Empirical Methods in Natural Language Processing*, pages 362–371. Association for Computational Linguistics.

Xiang Lin, Shafiq Joty, Prathyusha Jwalapuram, and Saiful Bari. 2019. A unified linear-time framework for sentence-level discourse parsing. In *Proceedings of the 56th Annual Meeting of the Association for Computational Linguistics*, ACL'19, pages xx–xx, Florence, Italy. ACL.

Ziheng Lin, Hwee Tou Ng, and Min-Yen Kan. 2011. Automatically evaluating text coherence using discourse relations. In *Proceedings of the 49th Annual Meeting of the Association for Computational Linguistics: Human Language Technologies - Volume 1*, HLT '11, pages 997–1006, Portland, Oregon. Association for Computational Linguistics.

Mohsen Mesgar and Michael Strube. 2018. A neural local coherence model for text quality assessment. In *Proceedings of the 2018 Conference on Empirical Methods in Natural Language Processing*, pages 4328–4339, Brussels, Belgium. Association for Computational Linguistics.

Tasnim Mohiuddin, Shafiq Joty, and Dat Nguyen. 2018. Coherence Modeling of Asynchronous Conversations: A Neural Entity Grid Approach. In *Proceedings of the 56th Annual Meeting of the Association for Computational Linguistics*, ACL'18, pages xx–xx, Melbourne, Australia. Association for Computational Linguistics.

Tasnim Mohiuddin, Thanh-Tung Nguyen, and Shafiq Joty. 2019. Adaptation of hierarchical structured models for speech act recognition in asynchronous conversation. In *Proceedings of the North American Chapter of the Association for Computational Linguistics: Human Language Technologies*, NAACL'19, pages xx–xx, Minneapolis, USA. ACL.

Mathieu Morey, Philippe Muller, and Nicholas Asher. 2017. How much progress have we made on RST discourse parsing? a replication study of recent results on the RST-DT. In *Proceedings of the 2017 Conference on Empirical Methods in Natural Language Processing*, pages 1319–1324, Copenhagen, Denmark. Association for Computational Linguistics.

Bita Nejat, Giuseppe Carenini, and Raymond Ng. 2017. Exploring joint neural model for sentence level discourse parsing and sentiment analysis. In *Proceedings of the 18th Annual SIGdial Meeting on Discourse and Dialogue*, pages 289–298. Association for Computational Linguistics.

Michael J. Paul. 2012. Mixed Membership Markov Models for Unsupervised Conversation Modeling. In *Proceedings of the 2012 Joint Conference on Empirical Methods in Natural Language Processing and Computational Natural Language Learning*, EMNLP-CoNLL '12, pages 94–104, Stroudsburg, PA, USA. ACL.

Emily Pitler and Ani Nenkova. 2008. Revisiting readability: A unified framework for predicting text quality. In *Proceedings of the 2008 Conference on Empirical Methods in Natural Language Processing*, pages 186–195, Honolulu, Hawaii. Association for Computational Linguistics.

Emily Pitler and Ani Nenkova. 2009. Using syntax to disambiguate explicit discourse connectives in text. In *Proceedings of the ACL-IJCNLP 2009 Conference Short Papers*, ACLShort '09, pages 13–16, Stroudsburg, PA, USA. Association for Computational Linguistics.

Rashmi Prasad, Aravind Joshi, Nikhil Dinesh, Alan Lee, Eleni Miltsakaki, and Bonnie Webber. 2005. The Penn Discourse TreeBank as a Resource for Natural Language Generation. In *Proceedings of the Corpus Linguistics Workshop on Using Corpora for Natural Language Generation*, pages 25–32, Birmingham, U.K.

Alan Ritter, Colin Cherry, and Bill Dolan. 2010. Unsupervised Modeling of Twitter Conversations. In *Human Language Technologies: The 2010 Annual Conference of the North American Chapter of the Association for Computational Linguistics*, HLT '10, pages 172–180, LA, California. ACL.

Rico Sennrich. 2018. Why the time is ripe for discourse in machine translation. Invited talk at the 2nd Workshop on Neural Machine Translation and Generation.

D. Shen, Q. Yang, J-T. Sun, and Z. Chen. 2006. Thread detection in dynamic text message streams. In *Proceedings of the 29th annual international ACM SIGIR conference on Research and development in information retrieval*, SIGIR '06, pages 35–42, Seattle, Washington, USA. ACM.

Radu Soricut and Daniel Marcu. 2003. Sentence Level Discourse Parsing Using Syntactic and Lexical Information. In *Proceedings of the 2003 Conference of the North American Chapter of the Association for Computational Linguistics on Human Language Technology - Volume 1*, NAACL'03, pages 149–156, Edmonton, Canada. ACL.

A. Stolcke, N. Coccaro, R. Bates, P. Taylor, C. Van Ess-Dykema, K. Ries, E. Shriberg, D. Jurafsky, R. Martin, and M. Meteer. 2000. Dialogue Act Modeling for Automatic Tagging and Recognition of Conversational Speech. *Computational Linguistics*, 26:339–373.

Rajen Subba and Barbara Di Eugenio. 2009. An effective discourse parser that uses rich linguistic information. In *Proceedings of Human Language Technologies: The 2009 Annual Conference of the North American Chapter of the Association for Computational Linguistics*, pages 566–574. Association for Computational Linguistics.

Hongning Wang, Chi Wang, ChengXiang Zhai, and Jiawei Han. 2011a. Learning online discussion structures by conditional random fields. In *Proceedings of the 34th International ACM SIGIR Conference on Research and Development in Information Retrieval*, SIGIR '11, pages 435–444, New York, NY, USA. ACM.

Li Wang, Marco Lui, Su Nam Kim, Joakim Nivre, and Timothy Baldwin. 2011b. Predicting thread discourse structure over technical web forums. In *Proceedings of the Conference on Empirical Methods in Natural Language Processing*, EMNLP '11, pages 13–25, Stroudsburg, PA, USA. Association for Computational Linguistics.

Yi-Chia Wang, Mahesh Joshi, William W. Cohen, and Carolyn Penstein Ros. 2008. Recovering implicit thread structure in newsgroup style conversations. In *ICWSM*. The AAAI Press.

Yizhong Wang, Sujian Li, and Houfeng Wang. 2017. A two-stage parsing method for text-level discourse analysis. In *Proceedings of the 55th Annual Meeting of the Association for Computational Linguistics (Volume 2: Short Papers)*, pages 184–188, Vancouver, Canada. Association for Computational Linguistics.

Lin Ziheng, Hwee Tou Ng, and Min-Yen Kan. 2014. A pdtb-styled end-to-end discourse parser. *Natural Language Engineering*, 20(2):151184.

Computational Analysis of Political Texts: Bridging Research Efforts Across Communities

Goran Glavaš and **Federico Nanni** and **Simone Paolo Ponzetto**
Data and Web Science Group, University of Mannheim
{goran, federico, simone}@informatik.uni-mannheim.de

1 Introduction

The development and adoption of natural language processing (NLP) methods by the political science community dates back to over twenty years ago. In the last decade the usage of computational methods for text analysis has drastically expanded in scope and has become the focus of many social science studies, allowing for a sustained growth of the text-as-data community (Grimmer and Stewart, 2013). Political scientists have in particular focused on exploiting available texts as a valuable (additional) data source for a number of analyses types and tasks, including inferring policy positions of actors from textual evidence (Laver et al., 2003; Slapin and Proksch, 2008; Lowe et al., 2011, *inter alia*), detecting topics (King and Lowe, 2003; Hopkins and King, 2010; Grimmer, 2010; Roberts et al., 2014), and analyzing stylistic aspects of texts, e.g., assessing the role of language ambiguity in framing the political agenda (Page, 1976; Campbell, 1983) or measuring the level of vagueness and concreteness in political statements (Baerg et al., 2018; Eichorst and Lin, 2018).

Just like in many other domains, much of the work on computational analysis of political texts has been enabled and facilitated by the development of dedicated resources and datasets such as, the topically coded electoral programmes (i.e., the Manifesto Corpus) (Merz et al., 2016) developed within the scope of the Comparative Manifesto Project (CMP) (Werner et al., 2014; Mikhaylov et al., 2012) or the topically coded legislative texts annotated for numerous countries within the scope of the Comparative Agenda Project (Baumgartner et al., 2006; Bevan, 2019).

While political scientists have dedicated a lot of effort to creating resources and using NLP methods to automatically process textual data, they have largely done so in isolation from the NLP community. For example, *political text scaling* – one of the central tasks in quantitative political science, where the goal is to quantify positions of politicians and/or parties on a scale based on the textual content they produce – has not received any attention by the NLP community until last year, whereas it has been at the core of political science research for almost two decades. At the same time, NLP researchers have addressed closely related tasks such as election prediction (O'Connor et al., 2010), ideology classification (Hirst et al., 2010), stance detection (Thomas et al., 2006), and agreement measurement (Gottipati et al., 2013), all rarely considered in the same format by the text-as-data political science community. In summary, these two communities have been largely agnostic of one another, resulting in NLP researchers not contributing to relevant research questions in political science and political scientists not employing cutting-edge NLP methodology for their tasks.

The main goal of this tutorial is to systematize and analyze the body of research work on computational analysis of political texts from both communities. We aim to provide a gentle, all-round introduction to methods and tasks related to computational analysis of political texts. Our vision is to bring the two research communities closer to each other and contribute to faster and more significant developments in this interdisciplinary research area. To that effect, this tutorial presents a continuation of our efforts which started with a very successful cross-community event organized in December 2017 (Nanni et al., 2018). In parallel with this tutorial at the 57th Annual Meeting of the Association for Computational Linguistics (ACL 2019), we will give a complementary tutorial at the 5th International Conference on Computational Social Science (IC^{2}S^2 2019).

Proceedings of the 55th Annual Meeting of the Association for Computational Linguistics, pages 18–23
Vancouver, Canada, July 30 - August 4, 2017. ©2017 Association for Computational Linguistics
https://doi.org/10.18653/v1/P17

2 Tutorial Overview

This introductory tutorial aims to systematically organise and analyse the overall body of research in computational analysis of political texts. This body of work has been split between two largely disjoint research communities – researchers in natural language processing and researchers in political science – and the tutorial is designed bearing this in mind. We first explain the role that textual data plays in political analyses and then proceed to examine the concrete resources and tasks addressed by the text-as-data political science community. Continuing, we present the research efforts carried out by the NLP researchers. We close the tutorial by presenting text scaling, a challenging task that is at the center of the quantitative political science and has recently also attracted attention of NLP scholars. Accordingly, we divide the tutorial into the following four parts:

1. **Text as Data in Political Science.** We begin with an overview of the role that textual data has always played in political science research as a source for determining leader's positions (Winter and Stewart, 1977), campaign strategies (Petrocik, 1996), media attention (Semetko and Valkenburg, 2000), and crowd perception of the democratic process (Miller, 1990). We will further analyze the inherent difficulties in collecting political texts and political data in general and analyze crowdsourcing as an efficient and agile method for producing political data (Benoit et al., 2016).

2. **Resources and Tasks.** We then present computational research tasks based on textual data, which are relevant for the political science community (Grimmer and Stewart, 2013). We examine the type of applications and discuss the complex challenges currently faced, especially concerning cross-lingual and topic-based studies. We will analyze in detail the corpora developed within the scope of two major annotation projects: Comparative Manifesto Project (Werner et al., 2014; Mikhaylov et al., 2012) and Comparative Agendas Project (Baumgartner et al., 2006; Bevan, 2019). We will also describe other datasets, annotated corpora, gold standards, and benchmarks that are already promptly available (Bakker et al., 2015; Merz et al., 2016; Schumacher et al., 2016; Van Aggelen et al., 2017; Döring and Regel, 2019).

3. **Topical Analysis of Political Texts.** Next, we focus on a large body of work of topical analysis of political texts, covering unsupervised topic induction, including dictionary-based, topic-modelling and text segmentation approaches (Quinn et al., 2006, 2010; Grimmer, 2010; Albaugh et al., 2013; Glavaš et al., 2016; Menini et al., 2017), as well as supervised topic classification studies (Hillard et al., 2008; Collingwood and Wilkerson, 2012; Karan et al., 2016). We will also cover more recent work on cross-lingual topic classification in political texts (Glavaš et al., 2017a; Subramanian et al., 2018). We will further emphasize topic classification models that exploit large manually anotated corpora from CMP (Zirn et al., 2016; Subramanian et al., 2017) and CAP (Karan et al., 2016; Albaugh et al., 2013) projects, which we cover in the previous part.

4. **Political Text Scaling.** Finally, we present a detailed overview of the task of political text scaling, which has the goal of inferring policy position of actors from textual evidence. After introducing the text scaling task, we will present in detail the traditional scaling models that operate on lexical text representations such as Wordscores (Laver et al., 2003) and WordFish (Slapin and Proksch, 2008; Lowe et al., 2011) as well as a more recent scaling approach that exploits latent semantic text representations (Glavaš et al., 2017b; Nanni et al., 2019). Furthermore, we will discuss the task of scaling multilingual text collections, presenting potential approaches and inherent issues. We conclude the tutorial with a short discussion of key challenges and foreseeable future developments in computational analysis of political texts.

3 Tutorial Outline

Part I: Text-as-Data in Political Science (*30 min*)

- Quick introduction to quantitative methods in political science
- Reliability and suitability of textual data for political analyses
- Constructing corpora of political texts
- Crowdsourcing political data: advantages and potential pitfalls

Part II: Resources and Tasks *(30 minutes)*

- Overview of computational analysis of political texts in the political science community
- International annotation projects: Comparative Manifesto Project (CMP) and Comparative Agendas Project (CAP)
- Other large collection of political texts (EuroParl, UK Hansard Corpus, etc.) and associated tasks

Part III: Topical Analysis of Political Texts *(60 minutes)*

- Dictionary-based approaches to classification of political text
- Unsupervised topical analysis of political texts with topic models
- Models for supervised topic classification of political texts
- Hierarchical and fine-grained topic classification
- Cross-lingual topic classification

Part IV: Political Text Scaling and Conclusion *(60 minutes)*

- Lexical models for political text scaling: Wordscores and WordFish
- Text scaling using latent semantic text representations
- Policy dimensions in scaling: pitfalls and artefacts
- Cross-lingual scaling
- Conslusion: short discussion of key challenges and presumed future developments

4 Tutorial Breadth

In our previous work, we contributed to the research efforts on topic classification (Nanni et al., 2016; Zirn et al., 2016; Glavaš et al., 2017a), semantic scaling of political texts (Glavaš et al., 2017b) as well as (dis-)agreement detection in party manifestos (Menini et al., 2017). However, the key objective of this tutorial is to provide a comprehensive overview of recent and current research on computational analysis of political texts, both in NLP and political science communities. We estimate that at most one quarter of the tutorial will be dedicated to covering our own work.

5 Presenters

Goran Glavaš is an Assistant Professor for Statistical Natural Language Processing at the Data and Web Science group, University of Mannheim. He obtained his Ph.D. at the Text Analysis and Knowledge Engineering Lab (TakeLab), University of Zagreb. His research efforts and interests are in the areas of statistical natural language processing (NLP) and information retrieval (IR), with focus on lexical and computational semantics, multi-lingual and cross-lingual NLP and IR, information extraction, and NLP applications for social sciences. He has (co-)authored over 60 publications in the areas of NLP and IR, publishing at top-tier NLP and IR venues (ACL, EMNLP, NAACL, EACL, SIGIR, ECIR). He is a co-organizer of the TextGraphs workshop series on graph-based NLP. He is a research associate at the Collaborative Research Center SFB 884 "Political Economy of Reforms" where he participates in two projects.

Federico Nanni is a Post-Doctoral researcher in Political Text Analiysis at the Collaborative Research Center SFB 884 "Political Economy of Reforms" and at the Data and Web Science Group of the University of Mannheim. He obtained his Ph.D. in History of Technology from the University of Bologna. The focus of his research is on adopting (and adapting) Natural Language Processing methods for supporting studies in Computational Social Sciences and Digital Humanities. Currently, he works on developing new methods for cross-lingual topic detection and scaling in political texts. He actively works as a researcher on two projects of the Collaborative Research Center SFB 884 – Project C4: "Measuring a common space and the dynamics of reform positions: Non-standard tools, non-standard actors" and Project B6: "Nonparametric and nonlinear panel data and time series analysis".

Simone Paolo Ponzetto is Professor of Information Systems at the University of Mannheim and member of the Data and Web Science Group, where he leads the NLP and IR group. Simone obtained his Ph.D. from the Institute for Natural Language Processing, University of Stuttgart and has spent almost 15 years of service in the ACL community, enthusiastically contributing as reviewer, area chair and tutorial presenter at various *ACL events. His main research interests lie in the areas of knowledge acquisition, text understanding, and the application of NLP methods for research in the digital humanities and computational social sciences. Simone is currently a principal investigator of the Collaborative Research Center SFB 884 "Political Economy of Reforms" where he is a co-PI on two projects (Project C4: "Measuring a common space and the dynamics of reform positions: Non-standard tools, non-standard actors'; and Project B6: "Nonparametric and nonlinear panel data and time series analysis").

6 Target audience / prerequisites

This tutorial is designed for students and researchers in Computer Science and Natural Language Processing. We assume only a basic, graduate-level understanding of NLP problems and machine learning techniques for NLP, as commonly possessed by the typical ACL event attendee. No prior knowledge of computational social science or political science is assumed.

Prerequisites

- *Math:* Basic knowledge of linear algebra, graph theory, and numeric optimization.
- *Linguistics:* None.
- *Machine Learning:* The tutorial will not go into the basics of underlying machine learning models. Knowledge of basic (supervised) machine learning concepts is required.

7 Recommended reading list

1. Justin Grimmer and Brandon M. Stewart. 2013. Text as data: The Promise and Pitfalls of Automatic Content Analysis Methods for political texts.Political Analysis, 21(3): 267–297.

2. Michael Laver, Kenneth Benoit, and John Garry. 2003. Extracting Policy Positions from Political Texts Using Words as Data. American Political Science Review, 97(02): 311–331.

3. Jonathan B. Slapin and Sven-Oliver Proksch. 2008. A Scaling Model for Estimating Time-Series Party Positions from Texts. American Journal of Political Science, 52(3): 705–722.

8 Other Information

Tutorial type: Introductory.

Tutorial materials: All tutorial materials and other information related to the tutorial are available at: `https://poltexttutorial.wordpress.com`

Acknowledgments

The work on this tutorial is supported by the German Science Foundation (DFG) within the scope of activities of the Collaborative Research Center SFB 884: "Political Economy of Reforms".

References

Quinn Albaugh, Julie Sevenans, Stuart Soroka, and Peter John Loewen. 2013. The automated coding of policy agendas: A dictionary-based approach. In *Proc. of CAP Conf.*

Nicole Baerg, Dominik Duell, and Will Lowe. 2018. Central bank communication as public opinion: Experimental evidence. Work in Progress.

Ryan Bakker, Catherine De Vries, Erica Edwards, Liesbet Hooghe, Seth Jolly, Gary Marks, Jonathan Polk, Jan Rovny, Marco Steenbergen, and Milada Anna Vachudova. 2015. Measuring party positions in europe: The Chapel Hill expert survey trend file, 1999–2010. *Party Politics* 21(1).

Frank R Baumgartner, Christoffer Green-Pedersen, and Bryan D Jones. 2006. Comparative studies of policy agendas. *Journal of European Public Policy* 13(7).

Kenneth Benoit, Drew Conway, Benjamin E Lauderdale, Michael Laver, and Slava Mikhaylov. 2016. Crowd-sourced text analysis: Reproducible and agile production of political data. *American Political Science Review* 110(2).

Shaun Bevan. 2019. Gone fishing: The creation of the comparative agendas project master codebook. In Frank Baumgartner, Christian Breunig, and Emiliano Grossman, editors, *Comparative Policy Agendas: Theory, Tools, Data*, Oxford University Press.

James E Campbell. 1983. Ambiguity in the issue positions of presidential candidates: A causal analysis. *American Journal of Political Science* 27(2).

Loren Collingwood and John Wilkerson. 2012. Tradeoffs in accuracy and efficiency in supervised learning methods. *Journal of Information Technology & Politics* 9(3).

Holger Döring and Sven Regel. 2019. Party facts: A database of political parties worldwide. *Party Politics* 25(2).

Jason Eichorst and Nick Lin. 2018. Resist to commit: Concrete campaign statements and the need to clarify a partisan reputation. *The Journal of Politics* 81(1).

Goran Glavaš, Federico Nanni, and Simone Paolo Ponzetto. 2016. Unsupervised text segmentation using semantic relatedness graphs. In *Proc. of *SEM*.

Goran Glavaš, Federico Nanni, and Simone Paolo Ponzetto. 2017a. Cross-lingual classification of topics in political texts. In *Proc. of NLP+CSS*.

Goran Glavaš, Federico Nanni, and Simone Paolo Ponzetto. 2017b. Unsupervised Cross-Lingual Scaling of Political Texts. In *Proc. of EACL*.

Swapna Gottipati, Minghui Qiu, Yanchuan Sim, Jing Jiang, and Noah A. Smith. 2013. Learning topics and positions from debatepedia. In *Proc. of EMNLP*.

Justin Grimmer. 2010. A bayesian hierarchical topic model for political texts: Measuring expressed agendas in senate press releases. *Political Analysis* 18(1).

Justin Grimmer and Brandon M. Stewart. 2013. Text as data: The promise and pitfalls of automatic content analysis methods for political texts. *Political Analysis* 21(3).

Dustin Hillard, Stephen Purpura, and John Wilkerson. 2008. Computer assisted topic classification for mixed methods social science research. *Journal of Information Technology and Politics* 4(4).

Graeme Hirst, Yaroslav Riabinin, and Jory Graham. 2010. Party status as a confound in the automatic classification of political speech by ideology. In *Proc. of JADT*.

Daniel J Hopkins and Gary King. 2010. A method of automated nonparametric content analysis for social science. *American Journal of Political Science* 54(1).

Mladen Karan, Jan Šnajder, Daniela Sirinic, and Goran Glavaš. 2016. Analysis of policy agendas: Lessons learned from automatic topic classification of croatian political texts. In *Proc. of SIGHUM*.

Gary King and Will Lowe. 2003. An automated information extraction tool for international conflict data with performance as good as human coders: A rare events evaluation design. *International Organization* 57(3).

Michael Laver, Kenneth Benoit, and John Garry. 2003. Extracting policy positions from political texts using words as data. *American Political Science Review* 97(02).

Will Lowe, Kenneth Benoit, Slava Mikhaylov, and Michael Laver. 2011. Scaling Policy Preferences from Coded Political Texts. *Legislative Studies Quarterly* 36(1).

Stefano Menini, Federico Nanni, Simone Paolo Ponzetto, and Sara Tonelli. 2017. Topic-based agreement and disagreement in us electoral manifestos. In *Proc. of EMNLP*.

Nicolas Merz, Sven Regel, and Jirka Lewandowski. 2016. The manifesto corpus: A new resource for research on political parties and quantitative text analysis. *Research & Politics* 3(2).

Slava Mikhaylov, Michael Laver, and Kenneth R. Benoit. 2012. Coder reliability and misclassification in the human coding of party manifestos. *Political Analysis* 20(01).

William Lockley Miller. 1990. *How Voters Change: the 1987 British election campaign in perspective*. Oxford University Press.

Federico Nanni, Goran Glavaš, Simone Paolo Ponzetto, and Heiner Stuckenschmidt. 2019. Political text scaling meets computational semantics. Work in Progress.

Federico Nanni, Goran Glavaš, Simone Paolo Ponzetto, Sara Tonelli, Nicolò Conti, Ahmet Aker, Alessio Palmero Aprosio, Arnim Bleier, Benedetta Carlotti, Theresa Gessler, Tim Henrichsen, Dirk Hovy, Christian Kahmann, Mladen Karan, Akitaka Matsuo, Stefano Menini, Dong Nguyen, Andreas Niekler, Lisa Posch, Federico Vegetti, Zeerak Waseem, Tanya Whyte, and Nikoleta Yordanova. 2018. Findings from the hackathon on understanding euroscepticism through the lens of textual data. In *Proc. of ParlaCLARIN*.

Federico Nanni, Cäcilia Zirn, Goran Glavaš, Jason Eichorst, and Simone Paolo Ponzetto. 2016. TopFish: topic-based analysis of political position in US electoral campaigns. In *Proc. of PolText*.

Brendan O'Connor, Ramnath Balasubramanyan, Bryan R. Routledge, and Noah A. Smith. 2010. From tweets to polls: Linking text sentiment to public opinion time series. In *Proc. of ICWSM*.

Benjamin Page. 1976. The theory of political ambiguity. *American Political Science Review* 70(3).

John Petrocik. 1996. Issue ownership in presidential elections, with a 1980 case study. *American journal of political science* 40(3).

Kevin M Quinn, Burt L Monroe, Michael Colaresi, Michael H Crespin, and Dragomir R Radev. 2006. An automated method of topic-coding legislative speech over time with application to the 105th-108th us senate. In *Proc of. APSA*.

Kevin M Quinn, Burt L Monroe, Michael Colaresi, Michael H Crespin, and Dragomir R Radev. 2010. How to analyze political attention with minimal assumptions and costs. *American Journal of Political Science* 54(1).

Margaret E. Roberts, Brandon M. Stewart, Dustin Tingley, Christopher Lucas, Jetson Leder-Luis, Shana Kushner Gadarian, Bethany Albertson, and David G. Rand. 2014. Structural topic models for open-ended survey responses. *American Journal of Political Science* 58(4).

Gijs Schumacher, Martijn Schoonvelde, Denise Traber, Tanushree Dahiya, and Erik De Vries. 2016. Euspeech: a new dataset of eu elite speeches. In *Proc. of PolText*.

Holli A Semetko and Patti M Valkenburg. 2000. Framing european politics: A content analysis of press and television news. *Journal of communication* 50(2).

Jonathan B Slapin and Sven-Oliver Proksch. 2008. A scaling model for estimating time-series party positions from texts. *American Journal of Political Science* 52(3).

Shivashankar Subramanian, Trevor Cohn, and Timothy Baldwin. 2018. Hierarchical structured model for fine-to-coarse manifesto text analysis. In *Proc. of NAACL*.

Shivashankar Subramanian, Trevor Cohn, Timothy Baldwin, and Julian Brooke. 2017. Joint sentence-document model for manifesto text analysis. In *Proc. of ALTA*.

Matt Thomas, Bo Pang, and Lillian Lee. 2006. Get out the vote: Determining support or opposition from congressional floor-debate transcripts. In *Proc. of EMNLP*.

Astrid Van Aggelen, Laura Hollink, Max Kemman, Martijn Kleppe, and Henri Beunders. 2017. The debates of the european parliament as linked open data. *Semantic Web* 8(2).

Annika Werner, Onawa Lacewell, and Andrea Volkens. 2014. *Manifesto Coding Instructions: 5th fully revised edition*. Manifesto Project.

David Winter and Abigail Stewart. 1977. Content analysis as a technique for assessing political leaders. In *A psychological examination of political leaders*, New York: Free Press.

Cäcilia Zirn, Goran Glavaš, Federico Nanni, Jason Eichorts, and Heiner Stuckenschmidt. 2016. Classifying topics and detecting topic shifts in political manifestos. In *Proc. of PolText*.

Wikipedia as a Resource for Text Analysis and Retrieval

Marius Paşca
Google
1600 Amphitheatre Parkway
Mountain View, California 94043
mars@google.com

1 Tutorial Description

As a counterpart to expert-created knowledge resources such as WordNet or Cyc, non-expert users may collaboratively create large resources of unstructured or semi-structured knowledge, a leading representative of which is Wikipedia. Collectively, articles within Wikipedia form an easily-editable collection, reflecting an ever-growing number of topics of interest to Web users.

This tutorial examines the characteristics of Wikipedia relative to other human-curated resources of knowledge; and the role of Wikipedia and resources derived from it in text analysis and in enhancing information retrieval. Applicable text analysis tasks include coreference resolution (Ratinov and Roth, 2012), word sense and entity disambiguation (Ganea and Hofmann, 2017). More prominently, they include information extraction (Zhu et al., 2019). In information retrieval, a better understanding of the structure and meaning of queries (Hu et al., 2009; Pantel and Fuxman, 2011; Tan et al., 2017) helps in matching queries against documents (Ensan and Bagheri, 2017), clustering search results (Scaiella et al., 2012), answer (Chen et al., 2017) and entity retrieval (Ma et al., 2018) and retrieving knowledge panels for queries asking about popular entities.

2 Outline

1. Human-curated resources
   (a) Expert resources
   (b) Collaborative, non-expert resources
   (c) Hybrid resources
2. Knowledge within Wikipedia
   (a) Articles, infoboxes, links, categories
   (b) Resources derived from Wikipedia
3. Role in text analysis
   (a) Information extraction
   (b) Beyond information extraction
4. Role in information retrieval
   (a) Query and document analysis
   (b) Retrieval and ranking

A copy will be at http://tinyurl.com/acl19wi.

3 Presenter

Marius Paşca is a research scientist at Google in Mountain View, California. He graduated with a Ph.D. in Computer Science from Southern Methodist University in Dallas, Texas and an M.Sc. in Computer Science from Joseph Fourier University in Grenoble, France. Current research interests include factual information extraction from unstructured text and natural-language matching functions for information retrieval.

References

D. Chen, A. Fisch, J. Weston, and A. Bordes. 2017. Reading Wikipedia to answer open-domain questions. In *ACL 2017*.

F. Ensan and E. Bagheri. 2017. Document retrieval model through semantic linking. In *WSDM 2017*.

O. Ganea and T. Hofmann. 2017. Deep joint entity disambiguation with local neural attention. In *EMNLP 2017*.

J. Hu, G. Wang, F. Lochovsky, J. Sun, and Z. Chen. 2009. Understanding user's query intent with Wikipedia. In *WWW 2009*.

D. Ma, Y. Chen, K. Chang, and X. Du. 2018. Leveraging fine-grained Wikipedia categories for entity search. In *WWW 2018*.

P. Pantel and A. Fuxman. 2011. Jigs and lures: Associating web queries with structured entities. In *ACL 2011*.

L. Ratinov and D. Roth. 2012. Learning-based multi-sieve co-reference resolution with knowledge. In *EMNLP-CoNLL 2012*.

U. Scaiella, P. Ferragina, A. Marino, and M. Ciaramita. 2012. Topical clustering of search results. In *WSDM 2012*.

C. Tan, F. Wei, P. Ren, W. Lv, and M. Zhou. 2017. Entity linking for queries by searching Wikipedia sentences. In *EMNLP 2017*.

Q. Zhu, X. Ren, J. Shang, Y. Zhang, A. El-Kishky, and J. Han. 2019. Integrating local context and global cohesiveness for open information extraction. In *WSDM 2019*.

Proceedings of the 55th Annual Meeting of the Association for Computational Linguistics, page 24
Vancouver, Canada, July 30 - August 4, 2017.
https://doi.org/10.18653/v1/P17

Deep Bayesian Natural Language Processing

Jen-Tzung Chien
Department of Electrical and Computer Engineering
National Chiao Tung University, Hsinchu, Taiwan
jtchien@nctu.edu.tw

1 Introduction

This *introductory* tutorial addresses the advances in deep Bayesian learning for natural language with ubiquitous applications ranging from speech recognition (Saon and Chien, 2012; Chan et al., 2016) to document summarization (Chang and Chien, 2009), text classification (Blei et al., 2003; Zhang et al., 2015), text segmentation (Chien and Chueh, 2012), information extraction (Narasimhan et al., 2016), image caption generation (Vinyals et al., 2015; Xu et al., 2015), sentence generation (Li et al., 2016), dialogue control (Zhao and Eskenazi, 2016), sentiment classification, recommendation system, question answering (Sukhbaatar et al., 2015) and machine translation (Bahdanau et al., 2014), to name a few. Traditionally, "deep learning" is taken to be a learning process where the inference or optimization is based on the real-valued deterministic model. The "semantic structure" in words, sentences, entities, actions and documents drawn from a large vocabulary may not be well expressed or correctly optimized in mathematical logic or computer programs. The "distribution function" in discrete or continuous latent variable model for natural language may not be properly decomposed or estimated. This tutorial addresses the fundamentals of statistical models and neural networks, and focus on a series of advanced Bayesian models and deep models including hierarchical Dirichlet process (Teh et al., 2006), Chinese restaurant process (Blei et al., 2010), hierarchical Pitman-Yor process (Teh, 2006), Indian buffet process (Ghahramani and Griffiths, 2005), recurrent neural network (Mikolov et al., 2010; Van Den Oord et al., 2016), long short-term memory (Hochreiter and Schmidhuber, 1997; Cho et al., 2014), sequence-to-sequence model (Sutskever et al., 2014), variational auto-encoder (Kingma and Welling, 2014), generative adversarial network (Goodfellow et al., 2014), attention mechanism (Chorowski et al., 2015; Seo et al., 2016), memory-augmented neural network (Graves et al., 2014; Sukhbaatar et al., 2015), skip neural network (Campos et al., 2018), stochastic neural network (Bengio et al., 2014; Miao et al., 2016), predictive state neural network (Downey et al., 2017) and policy neural network (Mnih et al., 2015; Yu et al., 2017). We present how these models are connected and why they work for a variety of applications on symbolic and complex patterns in natural language. The variational inference and sampling method are formulated to tackle the optimization for complicated models (Rezende et al., 2014). The word and sentence embeddings, clustering and co-clustering are merged with linguistic and semantic constraints. A series of case studies and domain applications are presented to tackle different issues in deep Bayesian processing, learning and understanding. At last, we will point out a number of directions and outlooks for future studies.

2 Objective of tutorial

Owing to the current growth in research and related emerging technologies in machine learning and deep learning, it is timely to introduce this tutorial to a large number of researchers and practitioners who are attending ACL 2019 and working on statistical models, deep neural networks, sequential learning and natural language processing and understanding. To the best of our knowledge, there is no similar tutorial presented in previous ACLs. This three-hour tutorial will concentrate on a wide range of theories and applications and systematically present the recent advances in deep Bayesian learning which are impacting the communities of machine learning, natural language processing and human language technology.

Proceedings of the 55th Annual Meeting of the Association for Computational Linguistics, pages 25–30
Vancouver, Canada, July 30 - August 4, 2017.
https://doi.org/10.18653/v1/P17

3 Tutorial outline

- Introduction
  - motivation and background
  - probabilistic models
  - neural networks
  - modern natural language models
- Bayesian Learning
  - inference and optimization
  - variational Bayesian (VB) inference
  - Monte Carlo Markov chain (MCMC)
  - Bayesian nonparametrics (BNP)
  - hierarchical theme and topic model
  - hierarchical Pitman-Yor-Dirichlet proc.
  - nested Indian buffet process
- Deep Learning
  - deep unfolded topic model
  - gated recurrent neural network (RNN)
  - generative adversarial network (GAN)
  - memory-augmented neural network
  - sequence-to-sequence learning
  - convolutional neural network (CNN) (Coffee Break)
  - dilated recurrent neural network
  - attention network using transformer
- Deep Bayesian Processing and Learning
  - Bayesian recurrent neural network
  - variational auto-encoder (VAE)
  - variational recurrent auto-encoder
  - stochastic temporal convolutional net
  - stochastic recurrent neural network
  - regularized recurrent neural network
  - stochastic learning & normalizing flows
  - VAE with VampPrior
  - skip recurrent neural network
  - temporal difference VAE
  - Markov recurrent neural network
  - reinforcement learning & understanding
  - sequence GAN
- Summarization and Future Trend

4 Target audience

This tutorial will be useful to research students working in natural language processing and researchers who would like to explore machine learning, deep learning and sequential learning. The prerequisite knowledge includes calculus, linear algebra, probability and statistics. This tutorial serves the objectives to introduce novices to major topics within deep Bayesian learning, motivate and explain a topic of emerging importance for natural language understanding, and present a novel synthesis combining distinct lines of machine learning work.

5 Description of tutorial content

The presentation of this tutorial is arranged into five parts. First of all, we share the current status of researches and applications on natural language processing, statistical modeling and deep neural network (Bahdanau et al., 2014), and address the key issues in deep Bayesian learning for discrete-valued observation data and latent semantics. Modern natural language models are introduced to address how data analysis is performed from language processing to semantic learning, memory networking, knowledge mining and understanding. Secondly, we address a number of Bayesian models ranging from latent variable model to VB inference (Chien and Chueh, 2011; Chien, 2015b; Chien and Chang, 2014), MCMC sampling and BNP learning (Chien, 2016, 2015a, 2018; Watanabe and Chien, 2015) for hierarchical, thematic and sparse topics from natural language. In the third part, a series of deep models including deep unfolding (Chien and Lee, 2018), RNN (Hochreiter and Schmidhuber, 1997), GAN (Goodfellow et al., 2014), memory network (Weston et al., 2015; Chien and Lin, 2018; Tsou and Chien, 2017), sequence-to-sequence learning (Graves et al., 2006; Gehring et al., 2017), CNN (Kalchbrenner et al., 2014; Xingjian et al., 2015; Dauphin et al., 2017), dilated RNN (Chang et al., 2017) and attention network with transformer (Vaswani et al., 2017; Devlin et al., 2018) are introduced. The coffee break is arranged within this part. Next, the fourth part focuses on a variety of advanced studies which illustrate how deep Bayesian learning is developed to infer the sophisticated recurrent models for natural language understanding. In particular, the Bayesian RNN (Gal and Ghahramani,

2016; Chien and Ku, 2016), VAE (Kingma and Welling, 2014), variational recurrent auto-encoder (Chien and Wang, 2019), neural variational learning (Serban et al., 2017; Chung et al., 2015), stochastic temporal convolutional network (Aksan and Hilliges, 2019), neural discrete representation (Jang et al., 2017; van den Oord et al., 2017), recurrent ladder network (Rasmus et al., 2015; Prémont-Schwarz et al., 2017), stochastic recurrent neural network (Fraccaro et al., 2016; Goyal et al., 2017; Chien and Kuo, 2017), predictive state neural network (Downey et al., 2017), Markov recurrent neural network (Venkatraman et al., 2017; Kuo and Chien, 2018), reinforcement learning (Tegho et al., 2017), sequence GAN (Yu et al., 2017), and temporal difference VAE (Gregor et al., 2019) are introduced in various deep models. Enhancing the prior/posterior representation in variational inference is addressed (Rezende and Mohamed, 2015; Tomczak and Welling, 2018). These sophisticated models open a window to numerous practical tasks such as reading comprehension, sentence generation, dialogue system, question answering and machine translation. Variational inference methods based on normalizing flows (Rezende and Mohamed, 2015) and "variational mixture of posteriors" prior (VampPrior) (Tomczak and Welling, 2018) are addressed. Posterior collapse problem in variational sequential learning is compensated. In the final part, we spotlight on some future directions for deep language understanding which can handle the challenges of big data, heterogeneous condition and dynamic system. In particular, deep learning, structural learning, temporal and spatial modeling, long history representation and stochastic learning are emphasized. Slides of this tutorial are available at (http://chien.cm.nctu.edu.tw/home/acl-tutorial).

6 Instructor

Jen-Tzung Chien is now with the Department of Electrical and Computer Engineering, National Chiao Tung University, Taiwan, where he is currently the University Chair Professor. He held the visiting researcher position with the IBM T. J. Watson Research Center, Yorktown Heights, NY, in 2010. His research interests include machine learning, deep learning, natural language processing and computer vision. He served as the associate editor of the IEEE Signal Processing Letters in 2008-2011, the guest editor of the IEEE Transactions on Audio, Speech and Language Processing in 2012, the organization committee member of ICASSP 2009, the area coordinator of Interspeech 2012, EUSIPCO 2017-2019, the program chair of ISCSLP 2018, the general chair of MLSP 2017, and currently serves as an elected member of the IEEE Machine Learning for Signal Processing (MLSP) Technical Committee. He received the Best Paper Award of IEEE Automatic Speech Recognition and Understanding Workshop in 2011 and the AAPM Farrington Daniels Award in 2018. Dr. Chien has published extensively including the books "Bayesian Speech and Language Processing", Cambridge University Press, in 2015, and "Source Separation and Machine Learning", Academic Press, in 2018. He has served as the Tutorial Speaker for APSIPA 2013, ISCSLP 2014, Interspeech 2013, 2016, ICASSP 2012, 2015, 2017, COLING 2018, AAAI 2019, KDD 2019, and IJCAI 2019. (http://chien.cm.nctu.edu.tw/)

Acknowledgments

This work was partially supported by the Ministry of Science and Technology, Taiwan, under MOST 108-2634-F-009-003.

References

Emre Aksan and Otmar Hilliges. 2019. STCN: stochastic temporal convolutional networks. In *Proc. of International Conference on Learning Representations*, page 2019.

Dzmitry Bahdanau, Kyunghyun Cho, and Yoshua Bengio. 2014. Neural machine translation by jointly learning to align and translate. *arXiv preprint arXiv:1409.0473*.

Yoshua Bengio, Eric Thibodeau-Laufer, Guillaume Alain, and Jason Yosinski. 2014. Deep generative stochastic networks trainable by backprop. In *Proc. of International Conference on Machine Learning*.

David M. Blei, Thomas L. Griffiths, and Michael I. Jordan. 2010. The nested Chinese restaurant process and Bayesian nonparametric inference of topic hierarchies. *Journal of the ACM*, 57(2). Article 7.

David M. Blei, Andrew Y. Ng, and Michael I. Jordan. 2003. Latent Dirichlet allocation. *Journal of Machine Learning Research*, 3(3):993–1022.

Víctor Campos, Brendan Jou, Xavier Giró-i Nieto, Jordi Torres, and Shih-Fu Chang. 2018. Skip RNN: learning to skip state updates in recurrent neural networks. In *Proc. of International Conference on Learning Representations*.

William Chan, Navdeep Jaitly, Quoc Le, and Oriol Vinyals. 2016. Listen, attend and spell: A neural network for large vocabulary conversational speech recognition. In *Proc. of IEEE International Conference on Acoustics, Speech and Signal Processing*, pages 4960–4964.

Shiyu Chang, Yang Zhang, Wei Han, Mo Yu, Xiaoxiao Guo, Wei Tan, Xiaodong Cui, Michael Witbrock, Mark A Hasegawa-Johnson, and Thomas S Huang. 2017. Dilated recurrent neural networks. In *Advances in Neural Information Processing Systems*, pages 77–87.

Ying-Lang Chang and Jen-Tzung Chien. 2009. Latent Dirichlet learning for document summarization. In *Proc. of IEEE International Conference on Acoustics, Speech and Signal Processing*, pages 1689–1692.

Jen-Tzung Chien. 2015a. Hierarchical Pitman-Yor-Dirichlet language model. *IEEE/ACM Transactions on Audio, Speech, and Language Processing*, 23(8):1259–1272.

Jen-Tzung Chien. 2015b. Laplace group sensing for acoustic models. *IEEE/ACM Transactions on Audio, Speech, and Language Processing*, 23(5):909–922.

Jen-Tzung Chien. 2016. Hierarchical theme and topic modeling. *IEEE Transactions on Neural Networks and Learning Systems*, 27(3):565–578.

Jen-Tzung Chien. 2018. Bayesian nonparametric learning for hierarchical and sparse topics. *IEEE/ACM Transactions on Audio, Speech, and Language Processing*, 26(2):422–435.

Jen-Tzung Chien and Ying-Lan Chang. 2014. Bayesian sparse topic model. *Journal of Signal Processing Systems*, 74(3):375–389.

Jen-Tzung Chien and Chuang-Hua Chueh. 2011. Dirichlet class language models for speech recognition. *IEEE Transactions on Audio, Speech, and Language Processing*, 19(3):482–495.

Jen-Tzung Chien and Chuang-Hua Chueh. 2012. Topic-based hierarchical segmentation. *IEEE Transactions on Audio, Speech, and Language Processing*, 20(1):55–66.

Jen-Tzung Chien and Yuan-Chu Ku. 2016. Bayesian recurrent neural network for language modeling. *IEEE Transactions on Neural Networks and Learning Systems*, 27(2):361–374.

Jen-Tzung Chien and Kuan-Ting Kuo. 2017. Variational recurrent neural networks for speech separation. In *Proc. of Annual Conference of International Speech Communication Association*, pages 1193–1197.

Jen-Tzung Chien and Chao-Hsi Lee. 2018. Deep unfolding for topic models. *IEEE Transactions on Pattern Analysis and Machine Intelligence*, 40(2):318–331.

Jen-Tzung Chien and Ting-An Lin. 2018. Supportive attention in end-to-end memory networks. In *Proc. of IEEE International Workshop on Machine Learning for Signal Processing*, pages 1–6.

Jen-Tzung Chien and Chun-Wei Wang. 2019. Variational and hierarchical recurrent autoencoder. In *Proc. of IEEE International Conference on Acoustics, Speech and Signal Processing*, pages 3202–3206.

Kyunghyun Cho, Bart Van Merriënboer, Caglar Gulcehre, Dzmitry Bahdanau, Fethi Bougares, Holger Schwenk, and Yoshua Bengio. 2014. Learning phrase representations using RNN encoder-decoder for statistical machine translation. In *Proc. of Conference on Empirical Methods in Natural Language Processing*, pages 1724–1734.

Jan K. Chorowski, Dzmitry Bahdanau, Dmitriy Serdyuk, Kyunghyun Cho, and Yoshua Bengio. 2015. Attention-based models for speech recognition. In *Advances in Neural Information Processing Systems*, pages 577–585.

Junyoung Chung, Kyle Kastner, Laurent Dinh, Kratarth Goel, Aaron C Courville, and Yoshua Bengio. 2015. A recurrent latent variable model for sequential data. In *Advances in Neural Information Processing Systems*, pages 2980–2988.

Yann N. Dauphin, Angela Fan, Michael Auli, and David Grangier. 2017. Language modeling with gated convolutional networks. In *Proc. of International Conference on Machine Learning*, pages 933–941.

Jacob Devlin, Ming-Wei Chang, Kenton Lee, and Kristina Toutanova. 2018. BERT: Pre-training of deep bidirectional transformers for language understanding. *arXiv preprint arXiv:1810.04805*.

Carlton Downey, Ahmed Hefny, Byron Boots, Geoffrey J Gordon, and Boyue Li. 2017. Predictive state recurrent neural networks. In *Advances in Neural Information Processing Systems*, pages 6055–6066.

Marco Fraccaro, Søren Kaae Sø nderby, Ulrich Paquet, and Ole Winther. 2016. Sequential neural models with stochastic layers. In *Advances in Neural Information Processing Systems*, pages 2199–2207.

Yarin Gal and Zoubin Ghahramani. 2016. A theoretically grounded application of dropout in recurrent neural networks. In *Advances in Neural Information Processing Systems*, pages 1019–1027.

Jonas Gehring, Michael Auli, David Grangier, Denis Yarats, and Yann N Dauphin. 2017. Convolutional sequence to sequence learning. In *Proc. of International Conference on Machine Learning*, pages 1243–1252.

Zoubin Ghahramani and Thomas L. Griffiths. 2005. Infinite latent feature models and the Indian buffet process. In *Advances in Neural Information Processing Systems*, volume 18, pages 475–482.

Ian Goodfellow, Jean Pouget-Abadie, Mehdi Mirza, Bing Xu, David Warde-Farley, Sherjil Ozair, Aaron Courville, and Yoshua Bengio. 2014. Generative adversarial nets. In *Advances in Neural Information Processing Systems*, pages 2672–2680.

Anirudh Goyal, Alessandro Sordoni, Marc-Alexandre Côté, Nan Ke, and Yoshua Bengio. 2017. Z-forcing: Training stochastic recurrent networks. In *Advances in Neural Information Processing Systems 30*, pages 6713–6723.

Alex Graves, Santiago Fernández, Faustino Gomez, and Jürgen Schmidhuber. 2006. Connectionist temporal classification: Labelling unsegmented sequence data with recurrent neural networks. In *Proc. of International Conference on Machine Learning*, pages 369–376.

Alex Graves, Greg Wayne, and Ivo Danihelka. 2014. Neural Turing machines. *arXiv preprint arXiv:1410.5401*.

Karol Gregor, George Papamakarios, Frederic Besse, Lars Buesing, and Theophane Weber. 2019. Temporal difference variational auto-encoder. In *Proc. of International Conference on Learning Representations*.

Sepp Hochreiter and Jürgen Schmidhuber. 1997. Long short-term memory. *Neural Computation*, 9(8):1735–1780.

Eric Jang, Shixiang Gu, and Ben Poole. 2017. Categorical reparameterization with Gumbel-softmax. In *Proc. of International Conference on Learning Representations*.

Nal Kalchbrenner, Edward Grefenstette, and Phil Blunsom. 2014. A convolutional neural network for modelling sentences. In *Proc. of Annual Meeting of the Association for Computational Linguistics*, pages 655–665.

Diederik P Kingma and Max Welling. 2014. Auto-encoding variational Bayes. *arXiv preprint arXiv:1312.6114*.

Che-Yu Kuo and Jen-Tzung Chien. 2018. Markov recurrent neural networks. In *Proc. of IEEE International Workshop on Machine Learning for Signal Processing*, pages 1–6.

Jiwei Li, Will Monroe, Alan Ritter, and Dan Jurafsky. 2016. Deep reinforcement learning for dialogue generation. In *Proc. of Conference on Empirical Methods in Natural Language Processing*, pages 1192–1202.

Yishu Miao, Lei Yu, and Phil Blunsom. 2016. Neural variational inference for text processing. In *Proc. of International Conference on Machine Learning*, pages 1727–1736.

Tomáš Mikolov, Martin Karafiát, Lukáš Burget, Jan Černocký, and Sanjeev Khudanpur. 2010. Recurrent neural network based language model. In *Proc. of Annual Conference of International Speech Communication Association*, pages 1045–1048.

Volodymyr Mnih, Koray Kavukcuoglu, David Silver, Andrei A Rusu, Joel Veness, Marc G Bellemare, Alex Graves, Martin Riedmiller, Andreas K Fidjeland, Georg Ostrovski, et al. 2015. Human-level control through deep reinforcement learning. *Nature*, 518(7540):529–533.

Karthik Narasimhan, Adam Yala, and Regina Barzilay. 2016. Improving information extraction by acquiring external evidence with reinforcement learning. In *Proc. of Conference on Empirical Methods in Natural Language Processing*, pages 2355–2365.

Aaron van den Oord, Oriol Vinyals, and Koray Kavukcuoglu. 2017. Neural discrete representation learning. In *Advances in Neural Information Processing Systems*, pages 6309–6318.

Isabeau Prémont-Schwarz, Alexander Ilin, Tele Hao, Antti Rasmus, Rinu Boney, and Harri Valpola. 2017. Recurrent ladder networks. In *Advances in Neural Information Processing Systems*, pages 6011–6021.

Antti Rasmus, Mathias Berglund, Mikko Honkala, Harri Valpola, and Tapani Raiko. 2015. Semi-supervised learning with ladder networks. In *Advances in Neural Information Processing Systems*, pages 3546–3554.

Danilo Jimenez Rezende and Shakir Mohamed. 2015. Variational inference with normalizing flows. In *Proc. of International Conference on Machine Learning*, pages 1530–1538.

Danilo Jimenez Rezende, Shakir Mohamed, and Daan Wierstra. 2014. Stochastic backpropagation and approximate inference in deep generative models. In *Proc. of International Conference on Machine Learning*, pages 1278–1286.

George Saon and Jen-Tzung Chien. 2012. Large-vocabulary continuous speech recognition systems: A look at some recent advances. *IEEE Signal Processing Magazine*, 29(6):18–33.

Minjoon Seo, Aniruddha Kembhavi, Ali Farhadi, and Hannaneh Hajishirzi. 2016. Bidirectional attention flow for machine comprehension. *arXiv preprint arXiv:1611.01603*.

Iulian V. Serban, Alessandro Sordoni, Ryan Lowe, Laurent Charlin, Joelle Pineau, Aaron Courville, and Yoshua Bengio. 2017. A hierarchical latent variable encoder-decoder model for generating dialogues. In *Proc. of AAAI Conference on Artificial Intelligence*, pages 3295–3301.

Sainbayar Sukhbaatar, Arthur Szlam, Jason Weston, and Rob Fergus. 2015. End-to-end memory networks. In *Advances in Neural Information Processing Systems*, pages 2440–2448.

Ilya Sutskever, Oriol Vinyals, and Quoc V Le. 2014. Sequence to sequence learning with neural networks. In *Advances in Neural Information Processing Systems*, pages 3104–3112. .

Christopher Tegho, Paweł Budzianowski, and Milica Gašić. 2017. Uncertainty estimates for efficient neural network-based dialogue policy optimisation. *arXiv preprint arXiv:1711.11486*.

Yee Whye Teh. 2006. A hierarchical Bayesian language model based on Pitman-Yor processes. In *Proc. of International Conference on Computational Linguistics and Annual Meeting of the Association for Computational Linguistics*, pages 985–992.

Yee Whye Teh, Michael I. Jordan, Matthew J. Beal, and David M. Blei. 2006. Hierarchical Dirichlet process. *Journal of the American Statistical Association*, 101(476):1566–1581.

Jakub Tomczak and Max Welling. 2018. VAE with a VampPrior. In *International Conference on Artificial Intelligence and Statistics*, pages 1214–1223.

Kai-Wei Tsou and Jen-Tzung Chien. 2017. Memory augmented neural network for source separation. In *Proc. of IEEE International Workshop on Machine Learning for Signal Processing*, pages 1–6.

Aaron Van Den Oord, Sander Dieleman, Heiga Zen, Karen Simonyan, Oriol Vinyals, Alex Graves, Nal Kalchbrenner, Andrew Senior, and Koray Kavukcuoglu. 2016. Wavenet: A generative model for raw audio. *arXiv preprint arXiv:1609.03499*.

Ashish Vaswani, Noam Shazeer, Niki Parmar, Jakob Uszkoreit, Llion Jones, Aidan N Gomez, Ł ukasz Kaiser, and Illia Polosukhin. 2017. Attention is all you need. In *Advances in Neural Information Processing Systems*, pages 5998–6008.

Arun Venkatraman, Nicholas Rhinehart, Wen Sun, Lerrel Pinto, Martial Hebert, Byron Boots, Kris Kitani, and J Bagnell. 2017. Predictive-state decoders: Encoding the future into recurrent networks. In *Advances in Neural Information Processing Systems*, pages 1172–1183.

Oriol Vinyals, Alexander Toshev, Samy Bengio, and Dumitru Erhan. 2015. Show and tell: A neural image caption generator. In *Proc. of IEEE Conference on Computer Vision and Pattern Recognition*, pages 3156–3164.

Shinji Watanabe and Jen-Tzung Chien. 2015. *Bayesian Speech and Language Processing*. Cambridge University Press.

Jason Weston, Sumit Chopra, and Antoine Bordes. 2015. Memory networks. In *Proc. of International Conference on Learning Representation*.

Shi Xingjian, Zhourong Chen, Hao Wang, Dit-Yan Yeung, Wai-kin Wong, and Wang-chun Woo. 2015. Convolutional LSTM network: A machine learning approach for precipitation nowcasting. In *Advances in Neural Information Processing Systems*, pages 802–810.

Kelvin Xu, Jimmy Ba, Ryan Kiros, Kyunghyun Cho, Aaron Courville, Ruslan Salakhudinov, Rich Zemel, and Yoshua Bengio. 2015. Show, attend and tell: Neural image caption generation with visual attention. In *Proc. of International Conference on Machine Learning*, pages 2048–2057.

Lantao Yu, Weinan Zhang, Jun Wang, and Yong Yu. 2017. SeqGAN: Sequence generative adversarial nets with policy gradient. In *Prof. of AAAI Conference on Artificial Intelligence*, volume 31, pages 2852–2858.

Xiang Zhang, Junbo Zhao, and Yann LeCun. 2015. Character-level convolutional networks for text classification. In *Advances in Neural Information Processing Systems*, pages 649–657.

Tiancheng Zhao and Maxine Eskenazi. 2016. Towards end-to-end learning for dialog state tracking and management using deep reinforcement learning. *arXiv preprint arXiv:1606.02560*.

Unsupervised Cross-Lingual Representation Learning

Sebastian Ruder[1], **Anders Søgaard**[2], **Ivan Vulić**[3]
[1] DeepMind, London
[2] Department of Computer Science, University of Copenhagen
[3] Language Technology Lab, University of Cambridge
sebastian@ruder.io soegaard@di.ku.dk iv250@cam.ac.uk

1 Motivation and Objectives

Cross-lingual word representations offer an elegant and language-pair independent way to represent content across different languages. They enable us to reason about *word meaning in multilingual contexts* and serve as an integral source of knowledge for multilingual applications such as machine translation (Artetxe et al., 2018d; Qi et al., 2018; Lample et al., 2018b) or multilingual search and question answering (Vulić and Moens, 2015). In addition, they are a key facilitator of *cross-lingual transfer* and *joint multilingual training*, offering support to NLP applications in a large spectrum of languages (Søgaard et al., 2015; Ammar et al., 2016a). While NLP is increasingly more embedded into a variety of products related to, e.g., translation, conversational or search tasks, resources such as annotated training data are still lacking or insufficient to induce satisfying models for many resource-poor languages. There are often no trained linguistic annotators for these languages, and markets may be too small or premature to invest in such training. This is a major challenge, but cross-lingual modelling and transfer can help by exploiting observable correlations between major languages and low-resource languages.

Recent work has already verified the usefulness of cross-lingual word representations in a wide variety of downstream tasks, and has provided extensive model classifications in several survey papers (Upadhyay et al., 2016; Ruder et al., 2018b). They cluster *supervised* cross-lingual word representation models according to the *bilingual supervision* required to induce such shared cross-lingual semantic spaces, covering models based on word alignments and readily available bilingual dictionaries (Mikolov et al., 2013; Smith et al., 2017), sentence-aligned parallel data (Gouws et al., 2015), document-aligned data (Søgaard et al., 2015; Vulić and Moens, 2016), or even image tags and captions (Rotman et al., 2018). The current trend (or rather 'obsession') in cross-lingual word embedding learning, however, concerns models that require a tiny amount of supervision (i.e., *weakly-supervised alignment* models that require only dozens of word translation pairs) or no supervision at all (*fully unsupervised* models).[1] Such resource-light unsupervised methods are based on the assumption that monolingual word vector spaces are approximately isomorphic (Conneau et al., 2018a). Therefore, they require only monolingual data and hold promise to enable cross-lingual NLP modeling in the absence of any bilingual resources. As a consequence, they offer support to a wider array of language pairs than supervised models, and promise to deliver language technology to truly resource-poor languages and dialects. However, due to the strong assumption on the similarity of space topology, these models often diverge to non-optimal solutions, and their robustness is one of the crucial research questions at present (Søgaard et al., 2018).

In this tutorial, we provide a comprehensive survey of the exciting recent work on cutting-edge weakly-supervised and unsupervised cross-lingual word representations. After providing a brief history of supervised cross-lingual word representations, we focus on: **1)** how to induce weakly-supervised and unsupervised cross-lingual word representations in truly resource-poor settings where bilingual supervision cannot be guaranteed; **2)** critical examinations of different training conditions and requirements under which unsupervised algorithms can and cannot work effectively; **3)** more robust methods for distant language pairs that

[1]Learning unsupervised cross-lingual models has indeed taken the field by storm: there are 10+ papers on this very topic published in EMNLP 2018 proceedings alone, with even more papers available on arXiv.

Proceedings of the 55th Annual Meeting of the Association for Computational Linguistics, pages 31–38
Vancouver, Canada, July 30 - August 4, 2017.
https://doi.org/10.18653/v1/P17

can mitigate instability issues and low performance for distant language pairs; **4)** how to comprehensively evaluate such representations; and **5)** diverse applications that benefit from cross-lingual word representations (e.g., MT, dialogue, cross-lingual sequence labeling and structured prediction applications, cross-lingual IR).

We will introduce researchers to state-of-the-art methods for constructing resource-light cross-lingual word representations and discuss their applicability in a broad range of downstream NLP applications, covering bilingual lexicon induction, machine translation (both neural and phrase-based), dialogue, and information retrieval tasks. We will deliver a detailed survey of the current cutting-edge methods, discuss best training and evaluation practices and use-cases, and provide links to publicly available implementations, datasets, and pretrained models and word embedding collections.[2]

2 Tutorial Overview

Part I: Introduction We first present an overview of cross-lingual NLP research, situating the current work on unsupervised cross-lingual representation learning, and motivating the need for multilingual training and cross-lingual transfer for resource-poor languages with weak supervision or no bilingual supervision at all. We also present key downstream applications for cross-lingual word representations, such as bilingual lexicon induction and unsupervised MT (Lample et al., 2018b). These tasks will be used throughout the tutorial to analyze the performance of different methods.

Almost all of the work on unsupervised cross-lingual representation learning fall into the category of *mapping-based approaches* (Ruder et al., 2018b). Such approaches to cross-lingual learning learn mapping functions between pretrained monolingual word embedding spaces; this is in contrast with approaches based on joint learning, data augmentation, or grounding. We show that such approaches to cross-lingual learning, while so far unexplored, can also be unsupervised. We will put focus on a standardized two-step mapping-based framework (Artetxe et al., 2018a) that generalizes all mapping-based approaches, and analyze the importance of each component of the framework. The two-step framework decomposes unsupervised cross-lingual representation learning into initial seed induction and iterative supervised bootstrapping.

Part II: Unsupervised and Weakly Supervised Alignment as Initial Seed Induction + Iterative Supervised Alignment We will analyze the impact of seed bilingual lexicon size and quality (e.g., cognates, named entities, or shared numerals) on the quality of weakly supervised cross-lingual word representations. Unsupervised and weakly supervised approaches can be directly compared by compared the quality of the learned dictionary seeds (Parts III and IV) to using cognates, named entities, etc.

Part III: Adversarial Seed Induction The underlying modus operandi of all adversarial methods will be demonstrated on the example of the MUSE architecture (Conneau et al., 2018a); this is by far the most cited adversarial seed induction method. We will then present similar adversarial methods and discuss their modeling choices, implementation tricks, and various trade-offs. We will also present our own direct comparisons of various GAN algorithms (e.g., WGAN, GP-WGAN, and CT-GAN) within the MUSE framework.

Part IV: Non-Adversarial Seed Induction In the next part, we will present several non-adversarial alternatives for unsupervised seed induction based on convex relaxations, point set registration methods, and evolutionary strategies. We will again dissect all components of the unsupervised methods and point to minor, but important implementation tricks and hyper-parameters that often slip under the radar (e.g., vocabulary size, post-mapping refinements, preprocessing steps such as mean centering and unit length normalisation, selected semantic similarity measures, hubness reduction mechanisms). We will also introduce the newest research that extends these methods from bilingual settings to multilingual settings (with more than 2 languages represented in the same shared space).

Part V: Stochastic Dictionary Induction improves Iterative Alignment We will then discuss stochastic approaches to improve the iterative refinement of the dictionary. Stochastic dictionary induction was introduced in Artetxe et al. (2018b), and we show that this bootstrapping technique improves performance and robustness, and is the main reason Artetxe et al. (2018b) achieves state-of-the-

[2]Slides of the tutorial are available at `https://tinyurl.com/xlingual`.

art performance for many language pairs. This part of our tutorial explores variation of stochastic dictionary induction.

Part VI: Robustness and (In)stability Unsupervised methods rely on the assumption that monolingual word vector spaces are approximately isomorphic and there exists a linear mapping between the two spaces. This assumption is not true for many cases, which leads to degenerate or suboptimal solutions. The efficacy and stability of unsupervised methods relies on multiple factors such as: monolingual representation models, domain (dis)similarity, language pair proximity and other typological properties, chosen hyper-parameters, etc. In this part, we will analyze the current problems with robustness and stability of weakly-supervised and unsupervised alignment methods in relation to all these factors, and introduce latest solutions to alleviate these problems. We will provide advice on how to approach weakly-supervised and unsupervised training based on a series of empirical observations available in recent literature (Søgaard et al., 2018; Hartmann et al., 2018). We will also discuss the (im)possibility of learning non-linear mappings using either non-linear generators or locally linear maps (Nakashole, 2018).

We will **conclude** by providing publicly available software packages and implementations, as well as available training datasets and evaluation protocols and systems. We will also list current state-of-the-art results on standard evaluation datasets, and sketch future research paths.

3 Outline

Part I: Introduction: Motivating and situating cross-lingual word representation learning; presentation of mapping-based approaches *(30 minutes)*

- Current challenges in cross-lingual NLP. NLP for resource-poor languages.
- Bilingual data and cross-lingual supervision. Why do we need weakly supervised and unsupervised cross-lingual representation learning?
- Bilingual supervision and typology of supervised cross-lingual representation models.
- Learning with word-level supervision: mapping-based approaches.

Part II: Unsupervised and Weakly Supervised Alignment as Initial Seed Induction + Iterative Supervised Alignment *(30 minutes)*

- A general framework for mapping-based approaches.
- Importance of seed bilingual lexicons.
- Learning alignment with weak supervision: small seed lexicons, shared words, numerals.

Part III: Adversarial Seed Induction *(30 minutes)*

- Fully unsupervised models using adversarial training; MUSE and related approaches.

Part IV: Non-Adversarial Seed Induction *(25 minutes)*

- Fully unsupervised models using optimal transport, Wasserstein distance, Sinkhorn distance, and other alternatives.
- Importance of minor technical "tricks": pre-mapping and post-mapping steps: length normalisation, mean centering, whitening and de-whitening, making the methods more robust

Part V: Stochastic Dictionary Induction improves Iterative Alignment *(15 minutes)*

- An overview of methods to improve iterative refinement of the dictionary.

Part VI: Robustness and (In)stability *(35 minutes)*

- Impact of language similarity and typological properties.
- Impact of chosen monolingual models, domain similarity, and hyper-parameters.
- Convergence criteria, possible and impossible setups for unsupervised methods.
- How to build more robust and more stable unsupervised methods?

Discussion and Final Remarks *(15 minutes)*

- Towards cross-lingual contextualised word embeddings.
- Publicly available software and training data.
- Publicly available evaluation systems.
- Concluding remarks, remaining challenges, future work, a short discussion.

4 Tutorial Breadth

Based on the representative set of papers listed in the selected bibliography, we anticipate that the 75%-80% of the tutorial will cover other people's work, while the rest concerns the work where at least one of the three presenters has been actively involved in. Note that the three presenters have been the main authors of the recent book on cross-lingual word representations which aimed at making a systematic overview of the field.

5 Prerequisites

- *Machine Learning*: Basic knowledge of common neural network components like word embeddings, RNNs, CNNs, denoising autoencoders, and encoder-decoder models.
- *Computational Linguistics*: Familiarity with standard NLP tasks such as machine translation.

6 Presenters

Ivan Vulić, PhD, Senior Research Associate, Language Technology Lab, University of Cambridge. 9 West Road, CB3 9DP, Cambridge, UK; Senior Scientist, PolyAI, London, UK. `iv250@cam.ac.uk`. Ivan is interested in representation learning, distributional, lexical, and multi-modal semantics in monolingual and multilingual contexts, and transfer learning for enabling cross-lingual NLP applications. His work has been published at top-tier *ACL and *IR conferences. Ivan co-lectured a tutorial on multilingual topic models and applications at ECIR 2013 and WSDM 2014, a tutorial on cross-lingual word representations at EMNLP 2017, and a tutorial on language understanding for conversational AI at NAACL 2018. He also co-organised a workshop on Vision and Language at EMNLP 2015 and co-organises the ACL 2019 workshop on linguistic typology for cross-lingual NLP. He serves as an area chair for the multilinguality track at NAACL 2019 and word-level semantics at ACL 2019.

Sebastian Ruder is a research scientist at DeepMind. His research focuses on transfer learning in NLP and transferring models to low-resource languages. He has published widely read reviews of related areas, co-organised the NLP Session at the Deep Learning Indaba 2018, and co-organises the ACL 2019 workshop on representation learning and the European NLP Summit 2019 (EurNLP-2019).

Anders Søgaard, PhD, Dr.Phil, Full Professor in NLP and Machine Learning, Department of Computer Science, University of Copenhagen. `soegaard@di.ku.dk`. Anders is interested in machine learning for NLP. He currently holds a Google Focused Research Award and a Facebook Research Award and has won best paper awards at NAACL, EACL, CoNLL and *SEM. He has previously given tutorials at COLING and EMNLP, as well as an ESSLLI course. He has been an area chair of many top NLP/AI conferences.

The presenters have recently published a handbook for Morgan & Claypool on *cross-lingual word embeddings*.

7 Other Important Information

Previous Tutorial Editions The EMNLP 2017 tutorial on cross-lingual word embeddings presented much of the earlier work from 2013-2016 that require large amounts of parallel data (i.e., supervised cross-lingual representations). In contrast, this tutorial focuses on cutting-edge unsupervised and weakly supervised approaches from the period of 2016-2018, which will be highly relevant to the audience, and will provide a complete overview of the current cutting-edge research in the field.

Acknowledgments

The work of IV is supported by the ERC Consolidator Grant LEXICAL (no 648909) awarded to Anna Korhonen at the University of Cambridge.

Selected Bibliography

Oliver Adams, Adam Makarucha, Graham Neubig, Steven Bird, and Trevor Cohn. 2017. Cross-lingual word embeddings for low-resource language modeling. In *Proceedings of EACL*, pages 937–947.

Jean Alaux, Edouard Grave, Marco Cuturi, and Armand Joulin. 2018. Unsupervised hyperalignment for multilingual word embeddings. *CoRR*, abs/1811.01124.

Hanan Aldarmaki, Mahesh Mohan, and Mona Diab. 2018. Unsupervised word mapping using structural similarities in monolingual embeddings. *Transactions of the ACL*, 6:185–196.

David Alvarez-Melis and Tommi Jaakkola. 2018. Gromov-Wasserstein alignment of word embedding spaces. In *Proceedings of EMNLP*, pages 1881–1890.

David Alvarez-Melis, Tommi S. Jaakkola, and Stefanie Jegelka. 2018. Structured optimal transport. In *Proceedings of AISTATS*, pages 1771–1780.

Waleed Ammar, George Mulcaire, Miguel Ballesteros, Chris Dyer, and Noah Smith. 2016a. Many languages, one parser. *Transactions of the ACL*, 4:431–444.

Waleed Ammar, George Mulcaire, Yulia Tsvetkov, Guillaume Lample, Chris Dyer, and Noah A. Smith. 2016b. Massively multilingual word embeddings. *CoRR*, abs/1602.01925.

Mikel Artetxe, Gorka Labaka, and Eneko Agirre. 2016. Learning principled bilingual mappings of word embeddings while preserving monolingual invariance. In *Proceedings of EMNLP*, pages 2289–2294.

Mikel Artetxe, Gorka Labaka, and Eneko Agirre. 2017. Learning bilingual word embeddings with (almost) no bilingual data. In *Proceedings of ACL*, pages 451–462.

Mikel Artetxe, Gorka Labaka, and Eneko Agirre. 2018a. Generalizing and improving bilingual word embedding mappings with a multi-step framework of linear transformations. In *Proceedings of AAAI*, pages 5012–5019.

Mikel Artetxe, Gorka Labaka, and Eneko Agirre. 2018b. A robust self-learning method for fully unsupervised cross-lingual mappings of word embeddings. In *Proceedings of ACL*, pages 789–798.

Mikel Artetxe, Gorka Labaka, and Eneko Agirre. 2018c. Unsupervised statistical machine translation. In *Proceedings of EMNLP*, pages 3632–3642.

Mikel Artetxe, Gorka Labaka, Eneko Agirre, and Kyunghyun Cho. 2018d. Unsupervised neural machine translation. In *Proceedings of ICLR*.

Antonio Valerio Miceli Barone. 2016. Towards cross-lingual distributed representations without parallel text trained with adversarial autoencoders. In *Proceedings of the 1st Workshop on Representation Learning for NLP*, pages 121–126.

Piotr Bojanowski, Edouard Grave, Armand Joulin, and Tomas Mikolov. 2017. Enriching word vectors with subword information. *Transactions of the ACL*, 5:135–146.

Chloé Braud, Ophélie Lacroix, and Anders Søgaard. 2017. Cross-lingual and cross-domain discourse segmentation of entire documents. In *Proceedings of ACL*, pages 237–243.

Jose Camacho-Collados, Mohammad Taher Pilehvar, Nigel Collier, and Roberto Navigli. 2017. SemEval-2017 Task 2: Multilingual and cross-lingual semantic word similarity. In *Proceedings of SEMEVAL*, pages 15–26.

Xilun Chen, Ahmed Hassan Awadallah, Hany Hassan, Wei Wang, and Claire Cardie. 2018. Zero-resource multilingual model transfer: Learning what to share.

Xilun Chen and Claire Cardie. 2018. Unsupervised multilingual word embeddings. In *Proceedings of EMNLP*, pages 261–270.

Ta Chung Chi and Yun-Nung Chen. 2018. CLUSE: Cross-lingual unsupervised sense embeddings. In *Proceedings of EMNLP*, pages 271–281.

Alexis Conneau, Guillaume Lample, Marc'Aurelio Ranzato, Ludovic Denoyer, and Hervé Jégou. 2018a. Word translation without parallel data. In *Proceedings of ICLR (Conference Track)*.

Alexis Conneau, Ruty Rinott, Guillaume Lample, Adina Williams, Samuel Bowman, Holger Schwenk, and Veselin Stoyanov. 2018b. XNLI: Evaluating cross-lingual sentence representations. In *Proceedings of EMNLP*, pages 2475–2485.

Georgiana Dinu, Angeliki Lazaridou, and Marco Baroni. 2015. Improving zero-shot learning by mitigating the hubness problem. In *Proceedings of ICLR (Workshop Papers)*, volume abs/1412.6568.

Zi-Yi Dou, Zhi-Hao Zhou, and Shujian Huang. 2018. Unsupervised bilingual lexicon induction via latent variable models. In *Proceedings of EMNLP*, pages 621–626.

Yerai Doval, Jose Camacho-Collados, Luis Espinosa Anke, and Steven Schockaert. 2018. Improving cross-lingual word embeddings by meeting in the middle. In *Proceedings of EMNLP*, pages 294–304.

Philipp Dufter and Hinrich Schütze. 2018. A stronger baseline for multilingual word embeddings. *CoRR*, abs/1811.00586.

Philipp Dufter, Mengjie Zhao, Martin Schmitt, Alexander Fraser, and Hinrich Schütze. 2018. Embedding learning through multilingual concept induction. In *Proceedings of ACL*, pages 1520–1530.

Long Duong, Trevor Cohn, Steven Bird, and Paul Cook. 2015. Cross-lingual transfer for unsupervised dependency parsing without parallel data. In *Proceedings of CoNLL*, pages 113–122.

Long Duong, Hiroshi Kanayama, Tengfei Ma, Steven Bird, and Trevor Cohn. 2016. Learning crosslingual word embeddings without bilingual corpora. In *Proceedings of EMNLP*, pages 1285–1295.

Greg Durrett, Adam Pauls, and Dan Klein. 2012. Syntactic transfer using a bilingual lexicon. In *Proceedings of EMNLP*, pages 1–11.

Goran Glavaš and Ivan Vulić. 2018a. Discriminating between lexico-semantic relations with the specialization tensor model. In *Proceedings of NAACL-HLT*, pages 181–187.

Goran Glavaš and Ivan Vulić. 2018b. Explicit retrofitting of distributional word vectors. In *Proceedings of ACL*, pages 34–45.

Goran Glavaš, Robert Litschko, Sebastian Ruder, and Ivan Vulić. 2019. How to (properly) evaluate cross-lingual word embeddings: On strong baselines, comparative analyses, and some misconceptions. In *Proceedings of ACL*.

Denis Gordeev, Alexey Rey, and Dmitry Shagarov. 2018. Unsupervised cross-lingual matching of product classifications. In *Proceedings of the 23rd Conference of Open Innovations Association (FRUCT)*, pages 62:459–62:464.

Stephan Gouws, Yoshua Bengio, and Greg Corrado. 2015. BilBOWA: Fast bilingual distributed representations without word alignments. In *Proceedings of ICML*, pages 748–756.

Edouard Grave, Armand Joulin, and Quentin Berthet. 2018. Unsupervised alignment of embeddings with Wasserstein Procrustes. *CoRR*, abs/1805.11222.

Jiang Guo, Wanxiang Che, David Yarowsky, Haifeng Wang, and Ting Liu. 2015. Cross-lingual dependency parsing based on distributed representations. In *Proceedings of ACL*, pages 1234–1244.

Mareike Hartmann, Yova Kementchedjhieva, and Anders Søgaard. 2018. Why is unsupervised alignment of English embeddings from different algorithms so hard? In *Proceedings of EMNLP*, pages 582–586.

Tatsunori Hashimoto, David Alvarez-Melis, and Tommi Jaakkola. 2016. Word embeddings as metric recovery in semantic spaces. *Transactions of the ACL*, 4:273–286.

John Hewitt, Daphne Ippolito, Brendan Callahan, Reno Kriz, Derry Tanti Wijaya, and Chris Callison-Burch. 2018. Learning translations via images with a massively multilingual image dataset. In *Proceedings of ACL*, pages 2566–2576.

Geert Heyman, Bregt Verreet, Ivan Vulić, and Marie-Francine Moens. 2019. Learning unsupervised multilingual word embeddings with incremental multilingual hubs. In *Proceedings of NAACL-HLT*, pages 1890–1902.

Geert Heyman, Ivan Vulić, and Marie-Francine Moens. 2017. Bilingual lexicon induction by learning to combine word-level and character-level representations. In *Proceedings of EACL*, pages 1085–1095.

Yedid Hoshen and Lior Wolf. 2018. Non-adversarial unsupervised word translation. In *Proceedings of EMNLP*, pages 469–478.

Kejun Huang, Matt Gardner, Evangelos Papalexakis, Christos Faloutsos, Nikos Sidiropoulos, Tom Mitchell, Partha P. Talukdar, and Xiao Fu. 2015. Translation invariant word embeddings. In *Proceedings of EMNLP*, pages 1084–1088.

Lifu Huang, Kyunghyun Cho, Boliang Zhang, Heng Ji, and Kevin Knight. 2018. Multi-lingual common semantic space construction via cluster-consistent word embedding. In *Proceedings of EMNLP*, pages 250–260.

Pratik Jawanpuria, Arjun Balgovind, Anoop Kunchukuttan, and Bamdev Mishra. 2019. Learning multilingual word embeddings in latent metric space: A geometric approach. *Transactions of the ACL*.

Armand Joulin, Piotr Bojanowski, Tomas Mikolov, Hervé Jégou, and Edouard Grave. 2018. Loss in translation: Learning bilingual word mapping with a retrieval criterion. In *Proceedings of EMNLP*, pages 2979–2984.

Yova Kementchedjhieva, Sebastian Ruder, Ryan Cotterell, and Anders Søgaard. 2018. Generalizing Procrustes analysis for better bilingual dictionary induction. In *Proceedings of CoNLL*, pages 211–220.

Yunsu Kim, Jiahui Geng, and Hermann Ney. 2018. Improving unsupervised word-by-word translation with language model and denoising autoencoder. In *Proceedings of EMNLP*, pages 862–868.

Guillaume Lample, Ludovic Denoyer, and Marc'Aurelio Ranzato. 2018a. Unsupervised machine translation using monolingual corpora only. In *Proceedings of ICLR*.

Guillaume Lample, Myle Ott, Alexis Conneau, Ludovic Denoyer, and Marc'Aurelio Ranzato. 2018b. Phrase-based & neural unsupervised machine translation. In *Proceedings of EMNLP*, pages 5039–5049.

Angeliki Lazaridou, Georgiana Dinu, and Marco Baroni. 2015. Hubness and pollution: Delving into cross-space mapping for zero-shot learning. In *Proceedings of ACL*, pages 270–280.

Omer Levy, Anders Søgaard, and Yoav Goldberg. 2017. A strong baseline for learning cross-lingual word embeddings from sentence alignments. In *Proceedings of EACL*, pages 765–774.

Robert Litschko, Goran Glavaš, Simone Paolo Ponzetto, and Ivan Vulić. 2018. Unsupervised cross-lingual information retrieval using monolingual data only. In *Proceedings of SIGIR*, pages 1253–1256.

Stephen Mayhew, Chen-Tse Tsai, and Dan Roth. 2017. Cheap translation for cross-lingual named entity recognition. In *Proceedings of EMNLP*, pages 2536–2545.

Ryan McDonald, Slav Petrov, and Keith Hall. 2011. Multi-source transfer of delexicalized dependency parsers. In *Proceedings of EMNLP*, pages 62–72.

Tomas Mikolov, Quoc V. Le, and Ilya Sutskever. 2013. Exploiting similarities among languages for machine translation. *CoRR*, abs/1309.4168.

Tasnim Mohiuddin and Shafiq Joty. 2019. Revisiting adversarial autoencoder for unsupervised word translation with cycle consistency and improved training. In *Proceedings of NAACL-HLT*, pages 3857–3867.

Nikola Mrkšić, Ivan Vulić, Diarmuid Ó Séaghdha, Ira Leviant, Roi Reichart, Milica Gašić, Anna Korhonen, and Steve Young. 2017. Semantic specialization of distributional word vector spaces using monolingual and cross-lingual constraints. *Transactions of the ACL*, 5:309–324.

Tanmoy Mukherjee, Makoto Yamada, and Timothy Hospedales. 2018. Learning unsupervised word translations without adversaries. In *Proceedings of EMNLP*, pages 627–632.

Ndapa Nakashole. 2018. NORMA: Neighborhood sensitive maps for multilingual word embeddings. In *Proceedings of EMNLP*, pages 512–522.

Ndapa Nakashole and Raphael Flauger. 2018. Characterizing departures from linearity in word translation. In *Proceedings of ACL*, pages 221–227.

Ndapandula Nakashole and Raphael Flauger. 2017. Knowledge distillation for bilingual dictionary induction. In *Proceedings of EMNLP*, pages 2497–2506.

Yves Peirsman and Sebastian Padó. 2010. Cross-lingual induction of selectional preferences with bilingual vector spaces. In *Proceedings of NAACL-HLT*, pages 921–929.

Edoardo Maria Ponti, Ivan Vulić, Goran Glavaš, Nikola Mrkšić, and Anna Korhonen. 2018. Adversarial propagation and zero-shot cross-lingual transfer of word vector specialization. In *Proceedings of EMNLP*, pages 282–293.

Ye Qi, Devendra Sachan, Matthieu Felix, Sarguna Padmanabhan, and Graham Neubig. 2018. When and why are pre-trained word embeddings useful for neural machine translation? In *Proceedings of NAACL-HLT*, pages 529–535.

Guy Rotman, Ivan Vulić, and Roi Reichart. 2018. Bridging languages through images with Deep Partial Canonical Correlation Analysis. In *Proceedings of ACL*, pages 910–921.

Sebastian Ruder, Ryan Cotterell, Yova Kementchedjhieva, and Anders Søgaard. 2018a. A discriminative latent-variable model for bilingual lexicon induction. In *Proceedings of EMNLP*, pages 458–468.

Sebastian Ruder, Ivan Vulić, and Anders Søgaard. 2018b. A survey of cross-lingual embedding models. *Journal of Artificial Intelligence Research*.

Tal Schuster, Ori Ram, Regina Barzilay, and Amir Globerson. 2019. Cross-lingual alignment of contextual word embeddings, with applications to zero-shot dependency parsing. In *Proceedings of NAACL-HLT*, pages 1599–1613.

Sidak Pal Singh, Andreas Hug, Aymeric Dieuleveut, and Martin Jaggi. 2018. Wasserstein is all you need. *CoRR*, abs/1808.09663.

Karan Singla, Dogan Can, and Shrikanth Narayanan. 2018. A multi-task approach to learning multilingual representations. In *Proceedings of ACL*, pages 214–220.

Samuel L. Smith, David H.P. Turban, Steven Hamblin, and Nils Y. Hammerla. 2017. Offline bilingual word vectors, orthogonal transformations and the inverted softmax. In *Proceedings of ICLR (Conference Track)*.

Anders Søgaard, Željko Agić, Héctor Martínez Alonso, Barbara Plank, Bernd Bohnet, and Anders Johannsen. 2015. Inverted indexing for cross-lingual NLP. In *Proceedings of ACL*, pages 1713–1722.

Anders Søgaard, Sebastian Ruder, and Ivan Vulić. 2018. On the limitations of unsupervised bilingual dictionary induction. In *Proceedings of ACL*, pages 778–788.

Chen-Tse Tsai and Dan Roth. 2016. Cross-lingual wikification using multilingual embeddings. In *Proceedings of NAACL-HLT*, pages 589–598.

Shyam Upadhyay, Manaal Faruqui, Chris Dyer, and Dan Roth. 2016. Cross-lingual models of word embeddings: An empirical comparison. In *Proceedings of ACL*, pages 1661–1670.

Shyam Upadhyay, Manaal Faruqui, Gökhan Tür, Dilek Z. Hakkani-Tür, and Larry P. Heck. 2018a. (almost) zero-shot cross-lingual spoken language understanding. In *Proceedings of ICASSP*, pages 6034–6038.

Shyam Upadhyay, Nitish Gupta, and Dan Roth. 2018b. Joint multilingual supervision for cross-lingual entity linking. In *Proceedings of EMNLP*, pages 2486–2495.

Shyam Upadhyay, Yogarshi Vyas, Marine Carpuat, and Dan Roth. 2018c. Robust cross-lingual hypernymy detection using dependency context. In *Proceedings of NAACL-HLT*, pages 607–618.

Ivan Vulić and Anna Korhonen. 2016. On the role of seed lexicons in learning bilingual word embeddings. In *Proceedings of ACL*, pages 247–257.

Ivan Vulic and Marie-Francine Moens. 2013. A study on bootstrapping bilingual vector spaces from non-parallel data (and nothing else). In *Proceedings of EMNLP*, pages 1613–1624.

Ivan Vulić and Marie-Francine Moens. 2015. Monolingual and cross-lingual information retrieval models based on (bilingual) word embeddings. In *Proceedings of SIGIR*, pages 363–372.

Ivan Vulić and Marie-Francine Moens. 2016. Bilingual distributed word representations from document-aligned comparable data. *Journal of Artificial Intelligence Research*, 55:953–994.

Ivan Vulić, Nikola Mrkšić, and Anna Korhonen. 2017. Cross-lingual induction and transfer of verb classes based on word vector space specialisation. In *Proceedings of EMNLP*, pages 2536–2548.

Takashi Wada and Tomoharu Iwata. 2018. Unsupervised cross-lingual word embedding by multilingual neural language models. *CoRR*, abs/1809.02306.

Ruochen Xu, Yiming Yang, Naoki Otani, and Yuexin Wu. 2018. Unsupervised cross-lingual transfer of word embedding spaces. In *Proceedings of EMNLP*, pages 2465–2474.

Pengcheng Yang, Fuli Luo, Shuangzhi Wu, Jingjing Xu, Dongdong Zhang, and Xu Sun. 2018a. Learning unsupervised word mapping by maximizing mean discrepancy. *CoRR*, abs/1811.00275.

Zhen Yang, Wei Chen, Feng Wang, and Bo Xu. 2018b. Unsupervised neural machine translation with weight sharing. In *Proceedings of ACL*, pages 46–55.

Meng Zhang, Yang Liu, Huanbo Luan, Yiqun Liu, and Maosong Sun. 2016a. Inducing bilingual lexica from non-parallel data with earth mover's distance regularization. In *Proceedings of COLING*, pages 3188–3198.

Meng Zhang, Yang Liu, Huanbo Luan, and Maosong Sun. 2017a. Adversarial training for unsupervised bilingual lexicon induction. In *Proceedings of ACL*, pages 1959–1970.

Meng Zhang, Yang Liu, Huanbo Luan, and Maosong Sun. 2017b. Earth Mover's distance minimization for unsupervised bilingual lexicon induction. In *Proceedings of EMNLP*, pages 1934–1945.

Mozhi Zhang, Keyulu Xu, Ken-ichi Kawarabayashi, Stefanie Jegelka, and Jordan Boyd-Graber. 2019. Are girls neko or shojo? Cross-lingual alignment of non-isomorphic embeddings with iterative normalization.

Yuan Zhang, David Gaddy, Regina Barzilay, and Tommi Jaakkola. 2016b. Ten pairs to tag – Multilingual POS tagging via coarse mapping between embeddings. In *Proceedings of NAACL-HLT*, pages 1307–1317.

Yftah Ziser and Roi Reichart. 2018. Deep pivot-based modeling for cross-language cross-domain transfer with minimal guidance. In *Proceedings of EMNLP*, pages 238–249.

Advances in Argument Mining

Chris Reed
Centre for Argument Technology
University of Dundee, UK
c.a.reed@dundee.ac.uk

Katarzyna Budzynska
Institute for Philosophy & Sociology
Polish Academy of Sciences
Warsaw, Poland
budzynska.argdiap@gmail.com

1 Description

This course aims to introduce students to an exciting and dynamic area that has witnessed remarkable growth over the past 36 months. Argument mining builds on opinion mining, sentiment analysis and related to tasks to automatically extract not just what *people think, but* why *they hold the opinions they do. From being largely beyond the state of the art barely five years ago, there are now many hundreds of papers on the topic, millions of dollars of commercial and research investment, and the 6th ACL workshop on the topic will be in Florence in 2019. The tutors have delivered tutorials on argument mining at ACL 2016, at IJCAI 2016 and at ESSLLI 2017; for ACL 2019, we have developed a tutorial that provides a synthesis of the major advances in the area over the past three years.*

Argument and debate form cornerstones of civilised society and of intellectual life. Processes of argumentation run our governments, structure scientific endeavour and frame religious belief. Recognising and understanding argument are central to decision-making and professional activity in all walks of life, which is why we place them at the centre of academic pedagogy and practice; it's why such a premium is placed upon these skills; and it's why rationality is one of the very defining notions of what it is to be human.

As our understanding of how arguments are assembled, are interpreted and have impact has improved, so it has become possible to frame computational questions about how it might be possible for machines to model and replicate the processes involved in identifying, reconstructing, interpreting and evaluating reasoning expressed in natural language arguments. This, then, is argument mining: identifying that an argument is present, decomposing an argument into its constituent parts, determining how those parts are connected and structured – and how they connect with other arguments and argument parts – and finally, evaluating the quality of those connections. Thorough overviews are provided in, e.g., (Stede and Schneider, 2018; Lippi and Torroni, 2016) with a wide range of more detailed themes covered elsewhere, such as premise-conclusion recovery (Stab and Gurevych, 2017), types of argumentation pattern (Walton et al., 2008), relationships between semantic and argumentative structures (Becker et al., 2017), how ethos of speakers interacts with argument structure (Duthie and Budzynska, 2018) and automated assessment of argument persuasiveness (Carlile et al., 2018).

Growth. From just a handful of papers in print around 2010, argument mining has grown rapidly with Google Scholar now reporting around 2,000 articles mentioning the topic in their title. ACL, EMNLP and NAACL have included over 50 articles on argument mining in the past three years alone, in addition to the 92 articles published at the ACL workshop series on Argument Mining (co-founded by Reed). Argument mining has been building momentum both within the ACL community and further afield, with both specialist conferences (such as Computational Models of Argument, COMMA, co-chaired in 2018 by Budzynska) and generalist conferences (such as IJCAI) devoting increasing time to papers, workshops and graduate-level training on argument mining. The creation and publication of datasets has been an important contributor to the vitality of the field, with papers at LREC and in LRE increasing the breadth of this foundational aspect to the field (Abbott et al., 2016). By the same token, new SEMEVAL tasks have also started to set the goalposts and shape robust comparative evalua-

Proceedings of the 55th Annual Meeting of the Association for Computational Linguistics, pages 39–42
Vancouver, Canada, July 30 - August 4, 2017. ©2017 Association for Computational Linguistics
https://doi.org/10.18653/v1/P17

tions (https://competitions.codalab.org/competitions/17327).

Challenge. Argument mining is a particularly challenging task and is an exciting domain in which to work because it is increasingly clear that deep learning and distributional techniques alone are not delivering the same kind of successes that have been enjoyed in some other areas of NLP. Many labs working with algorithms for argument mining are finding that hybrid approaches that integrate rule-based and statistical methods are more likely to deliver the strongest performance. As a result, recent argument mining has been pushing the boundaries of approaches to NLP in general.

Argument mining in the press. The past year has seen a rapidly accelerating public profile for argument technologies in general, with Reed commissioned to produce articles that have appeared in Newsweek (arg.tech/newsweek) and on the BBC (arg.tech/bbcnews), and media events such as IBM's Project Debater launch (e.g., www.wired.com/story/now-the-computer-can-argue-with-you). The BBC too has commissioned technology that includes the first live deployment of argument mining (www.bbc.co.uk/taster/pilots/evidence-toolkit-moral-maze) in supporting identification of fake news. The tutorial will make use of these high-profile applications of argument mining to contextualise and motivate the topics covered.

2 Type

As argument mining has been covered at an ACL tutorial previously, in 2016. This tutorial is classified as 'Introductory' and the syllabus is designed to minimise preprequisites. We aim, however, to focus heavily on results from the past three years during which time significant progress has been made.

3 Outline

The tutorial is structured in two parts, each of which mixes lecturing with practical work. In the first part, we will cover theory of argument structure from (i) the basics in argumentation theory; through (ii) recent results in computational models of argument; to (iii) the latest (as yet largely unpublished) techniques that allow modelling of dialogical argumentation. To consolidate understanding of the material in each of these 20 minute blocks, the first part concludes with a 30 minute practical session in which students will get an opportunity to apply the theory to an example drawn from a real-life setting.

In the second part, we will cover techniques for argument mining from (i) straightforward application of machine learning techniques; through (ii) use of BiLSTMs in particular for exploiting sequence structure latent in argument presentation; to (iii) the development of hybrid approaches to argument mining. We will again encourage deep understanding from the students through a short practical implementation exercise making use of R.

The outline syllabus runs thus:

Part A: Foundations

- **A1** (20 mins). Theory of argument structure – linked, convergent, serial, divergent, rebut, undercut – indicators – enthymemes – logos, ethos, pathos.

- **A2** (20 mins). Semantic types – argumentation schemes – ADU segmentation – datasets, corpora and shared tasks.

- **A3** (20 mins). Argument in dialogue – Inference Anchoring Theory – reported speech – complex and implicit speech acts.

- **A4** (30 mins). Practical session: Analysing natural argument.

Break

Part B: Applications

- **B1** (20 mins). Simple machine learning. IOB schema for segmentation – classifiers for arg-nonarg – classifiers for premise-conclusion.

- **B2** (20 mins). Advanced machine learning. Word embeddings for argumentation schemes – BiLSTM models for argumentation sequence patterns.

- **B3** (20 mins). Hybrid approaches. Argument structure parsing – illocutionary structure parsing – dialogical priors.

- **B4** (30 mins). Practical session: Argument mining in R.

All materials will be made available at a dedicated tutorial website as they were for our ACL2016, IJCAI 2016 and ESSLLI 2017 tutorials.

This website will be located at `http://arg.tech/acl2019tut`.

4 Prerequisites

The tutorial is intended to be accessible to most ACL attendees, so has straightforward prerequisites:

- Basic familiarity with supervised machine learning techniques and the way they are employed and assessed
- Experience of using R will be an advantage, but is not required, for practical session B4.

Attendees are expected to have or to be working towards a PhD in computational linguistics or a closely cognate area, but no previous experience of academic investigation of argument is expected.

5 Tutors

Katarzyna Budzynska (Computational Ethos Lab, Polish Academy of Sciences, budzynska.argdiap@gmail.com, `www.computationalethos.org`). Katarzyna is an associate professor in philosophy at the National Polish Academy of Sciences and an associate professor in computing at the University of Dundee (UK). Her work focuses on communication structures of argumentation, dialogue and ethos. She has published two books and over 80 peer-reviewed papers including articles in journals such as *Artificial Intelligence*, *Association for Computing Machinery (ACM TOIT)* and *Synthese*. Katarzyna founded a national movement, the Polish School of Argumentation, and sits in the steering committees of a new initiative, the European Conference on Argumentation (`ecargument.org`), and the ArgDiaP Association for Argumentation, Dialogue and Persuasion (`argdiap.pl`). Most recently, she established her research group – the Computational Ethos Lab which develops innovative technologies to process the use of ethos in natural language in order to predict the results of presidential elections, detect trolls and cyber-bullies in social media, and uncover potential terrorist threats. With Villata, she delivered a tutorial on Argument Mining at IJCAI 2016, and with Reed an extensive week-long course at the 29th European Summer School in Logic, Language, and Information (ESSLLI2017).

Chris Reed (Centre for Argument Technology, University of Dundee, c.a.reed@dundee.ac.uk, `www.arg.tech`). Chris is Full Professor of Computer Science and Philosophy at the University of Dundee, where he heads the Centre for Argument Technology. Chris has been working at the overlap between argumentation theory and artificial intelligence for over twenty years, has won over £6m of funding from government and commercial sources and has over 200 peer-reviewed papers in the area (including papers in ACL, COLING, IJCAI, ECAI and AAAI) and five books. He has also been instrumental in the development of the Argument Interchange Format, an international standard for computational work in the area; he is spear-heading the major engineering effort behind the Argument Web; and he was a founding editor of the Journal of Argument & Computation. He was co-organiser of COMMA 2014, of the first ACL workshop on Argumentation Mining in 2014, was the chair of the third workshop on Argument Mining with ACL in 2016, and has recently won funding for a £1m project on the topic in collaboration with IBM. With Gurevych, Stein and Slonim, he delivered a tutorial on Argument Mining at ACL 2016 which was extremely well attended, and followed that with a course at ESSLLI 2017 with Budzynska.

Acknowledgments

Our work in developing this tutorial has been supported in part in the UK by EPSRC under grant EP/N014781/1.

References

Rob Abbott, Brian Ecker, Pranav Anand, and Marilyn A. Walker. 2016. Internet Argument Corpus 2.0: An SQL schema for dialogic social media and the corpora to go with it. In *Language Resources and Evaluation Conference (LREC)*, Portorož, Slovenia.

Maria Becker, Alexis Palmer, and Anette Frank. 2017. Semantic clause types and modality as features for argument analysis. *Journal of Argument and Computation*, 8(2):95–112.

Winston Carlile, Nishant Gurrapadi, Zixuan Ke, and Vincent Ng. 2018. Give me more feedback: Annotating argument persuasiveness and related attributes in student essays. In *Proceedings of the 56th Annual Meeting of the Association for Computational Linguistics*, pages 621–631. Association for Computational Linguistics.

Rory Duthie and Katarzyna Budzynska. 2018. A deep modular rnn approach for ethos mining. In *Proceedings of the Twenty-Seventh International Joint Conference on Artificial Intelligence, IJCAI-18*, pages 4041–4047.

Marco Lippi and Paolo Torroni. 2016. Argumentation mining: State of the art and emerging trends. *ACM Trans. Internet Technology*, 16(2):10:1–10:25.

Christian Stab and Iryna Gurevych. 2017. Parsing argumentation structures in persuasive essays. *Computational Linguistics*, 43(3):619–659.

Manfred Stede and Jodi Schneider. 2018. *Argumentation Mining*. Synthesis Lectures on Human Language Technologies. Morgan Claypool.

Douglas Walton, Chris Reed, and Fabrizio Macagno. 2008. *Argumentation Schemes*. Cambridge University Press.

Storytelling from Structured Data and Knowledge Graphs
An NLG Perspective

Abhijit Mishra Anirban Laha Karthik Sankaranarayanan Parag Jain Saravanan Krishnan
IBM Research
{abhijimi , anirlaha , kartsank , pajain34 , sarkris5}@in.ibm.com

1 Goal of the Tutorial

In this tutorial, we wish to cover the foundational, methodological, and system development aspects of translating structured data (such as data in tabular form) and knowledge bases (such as knowledge graphs) into natural language. The attendees of the tutorial will be able to take away from this tutorial, (1) the basic ideas around how modern NLP and NLG techniques could be applied to describe and summarize textual data in format that is non-linguistic in nature or has some structure, and (2) a few interesting open-ended questions, which could lead to significant research contributions in future.

The tutorial aims to convey challenges and nuances in translation structured data into natural language forms, data representation techniques, and domain adaptable solutions. Various solutions, starting from traditional rule based/heuristic driven and modern data-driven and ultra-modern deep-neural style architectures will be discussed, and will be followed by a brief discussion on evaluation and quality estimation. A significant portion of the tutorial will be dedicated towards unsupervised, scalable, and adaptable solutions, given that systems for such an important task will never naturally enjoy sustainable large scale domain independent labeled (parallel) data.

2 Tutorial Overview

Natural Language Generation (NLG) has undergone significant advancement in the recent past, and various NLG systems are being used for either *data-to-text* tasks (*e.g.* generating financial reports from tables, generating weather reports) or *text-to-text* tasks (*e.g.* summarizing news reports, text-style transfer).

Structured data and knowledge bases or knowledge graphs are a key machine representation mechanism used in a wide variety of domains to capture domain-specific knowledge. For example, 1) the financial performance of companies and industries in financial domain, or 2) information about chemical composition of drugs, patient records, *etc.* in healthcare domain, or 3) inventory records of products and their features in retail, are all captured with domain-specific KGs/KBs. For AI driven interaction applications, often times it is important to communicate the content being represented in such knowledge bases in the form of natural language (such as English). Take an example in question-answering setting in Financial domain where a question:

"*How did XYZ corp. perform compared to its competitors in North America in last 2 quarters?*" would query a DB/KG and retrieves a result set table containing the relevant financial performance numbers about revenues, profit margin, competitors, technology segments, quarterly breakdown, etc.. However, it is not just sufficient for an AI system to simply display such a table of numbers, but rather, go one step further and explain in plain natural language the key message that addresses the user's question, for example, by saying,

"*In the N.A. region, XYZ Corp's revenues in the Cloud segment increased by 11% to $8.9B in the last 2 quarters as compared to its key competitor Microsoft. However, in the Analytics segment its revenues declined by 3% while Microsoft revenues grew by 4% and that of other smaller players in Analytics increased much more (around 8%).*"

Another important use-case is *story-telling* from data such as report generation – for example in weather domain (localized weather reports), finance (company performance reports) or healthcare (patient reports).

Motivated by above, this first-of-its kind tutorial intends to provide the conceptual underpinnings of the natural language generation (NLG) from a variety of structured representations. We will discuss various NLG paradigms ranging from heuristics to the modern data-driven techniques that include end-to-end neural architectures. A brief overview of evaluation methods and output quality estimation techniques will also be provided.

Proceedings of the 55th Annual Meeting of the Association for Computational Linguistics, pages 43–48
Vancouver, Canada, July 30 - August 4, 2017.
https://doi.org/10.18653/v1/P17

3 Type of the tutorial

Cutting-edge : We believe this topic picked up steam in the recent years given the deluge of papers regarding *data-to-text*. To the best of our knowledge, this topic has not been covered in any ACL/EMNLP-IJCNLP/NAACL tutorial.

4 Content of the Tutorial

We plan to organize a three-hour tutorial based on the following content. We will make efforts to make the tutorial interactive by having quizzes at regular intervals and also we hope to accommodate questions in between:

4.1 PART-I

1. **Introduction to NLG from Structured data and Knowledge Bases (20 mins)**
    - Data-to-text and text-to-text paradigms
    - Motivation: Why is this problem is important
    - Challenges in structured data translation: Why known text-to-text methods can not be applied to this problem?
    - Roadmap of the tutorial
2. **Heuristic Driven Methods (20 mins)**
    - Rule-based approaches
    - Template-based approaches
    - Current industry solutions
    - Shortcomings of this paradigm
3. **Statistical and Neural Methods (30 mins)**
    - Probabilistic Generation Models
    - Context-free Grammar based Approaches
    - Three-phase Approach : Planning, Selection and Surface Realization
    - End-to-end Encoder Decoder Paradigm
    - seq2seq approaches with attention
4. **Evaluation Methods for NLG (10 mins)**
    - N-gram based methods : BLEU, ROUGE
    - Document similarity based methods
    - Task-specific evaluation
    - Human evaluation metrics

4.2 PART-II

1. **Hybrid Methods - More adaptable (20 mins)**
    - Structured data input formats
    - Canonicalization
    - Simple Language Generation
    - Ranking of simple sentences
    - Sentence Compounding
    - Coreference Replacement
2. **Role of Semantics and Pragmatics (15 mins)**
    - Role of Knowledge Graphs
    - Domain-specific ontologies
    - Reasoning and Inference in Generation
3. **Open Problems and Future Directions (20 mins)**
    - Structure-aware Generation
    - Theme/Topic based Generation
    - Argumentative Text Generation
    - Controllable Text Generation
    - Creative Text Generation
4. **Conclusion and Closing Remarks (15 mins)**

Below we provide a bit more details about each of the above proposed sections to be covered in this tutorial.

Introduction to NLG from Structured data and Knowledge Bases: According to (Nema et al., 2018), the approaches for NLG range from (i) rule based approaches (ii) modular statistical approaches which divide the process into three phases (planning, selection and surface realization) and use data driven approaches for one or more of these phases (iii) hybrid approaches which rely on a combination of handcrafted rules and corpus statistics and (iv) the more recent neural network based models. Recent availability of large-scale parallel datasets like WikiBio (Lebret et al., 2016), WebNLG (Gardent et al., 2017) have been like a catalyst for the recent research in NLG from structured data using data-driven neural models. However, modern NLG still faces challenges in various phases of content selection, surface realization and evaluation, as pointed out by Wiseman et al. (2017).

Heuristic Driven Methods: This paradigm was followed by early research in NLP and NLG (*e.g.*, (Dale et al., 2003; Reiter et al., 2005; Green, 2006; Galanis and Androutsopoulos, 2007; Turner et al., 2010)). They range from rule-based techniques to template-based techniques. Often these approaches involve choosing the right set of rules or retrieving the appropriate template for the generation task. Many popular industry solutions like Arria NLG[1] and Automated Insights[2] also follow this approach. As evident, there can only be a limited number of cases which can be handled by rules or that templates can cover. Hence, this approaches are not scalable or adaptable, paving the way for statistical approaches.

Statistical and Neural Methods: These approaches were formulated to alleviate some limitations of the earlier approaches. Some notable approaches are based on probabilistic language generation process (Angeli et al., 2010), context-free grammar based generation (Konstas and Lapata, 2012) and others (Barzilay and Lapata, 2005; Belz, 2008; Kim and Mooney, 2010). They popularized the three-phase paradigm by breaking the problem into three phases, namely, content planning, content selection and surface realization. The more recent neural approaches following the encoder-decoder paradigm, however, have tried to circumvent the three-phase approach by using a single-phase end-to-end architecture. This was mainly popularized by the advent of attention mechanism for seq2seq (Bahdanau et al., 2014), later followed by many (Mei et al., 2016; Lebret et al., 2016; Nema et al., 2018; Jain et al., 2018; Bao et al., 2018). However, these approaches are data-hungry and perform miserably on datasets from *unseen* domains (Gardent et al., 2017). Realizing this, some of the very recent works in data-to-text generation such as Wiseman et al. (2018) have focused on learning templates from corpora for neural NLG.

Evaluation Methods for NLG: Alongside discussion of methods for automatic generation of natural language, it is much needed to acquaint the participants about automatic evaluation metrics like BLEU(Papineni et al., 2002), ROUGE(Ganesan, 2018), METEOR(Banerjee and Lavie, 2005), among many others. Often, a different kind of evaluation is needed to measure the semantic relatedness which the above N-gram overlap based metrics may not always capture. In addition, for various NLG tasks, specialized metrics have been proposed like FleschKincaid for readability and SARI (Xu et al., 2016) for text simplification. However, the automatic metrics are not always enough to capture nuances like fluency, adequacy, coherence and correctness, which many NLG systems fallback on humans for evaluation.

Hybrid Methods: Some earlier approaches like (Langkilde and Knight, 1998; Soricut and Marcu, 2006; Mairesse and Walker, 2011) try to follow a combination of rules and corpus statistics to overcome the above shortcomings. In this portion of the tutorial, we are going to present a hybrid modular approach developed by us which can be broken down into three simple steps: (1) Canonicalization, (2) Simple Language Generation, and (3) Discourse synthesis and Language Enrichment. This has been developed in a domain-agnostic way without the need for any parallel corpora to train. This is not very data dependent and adaptable to various unseen domains as the generation steps are mostly restricted to linguistic aspects. We believe this is how the data-to-text generation research should progress.

Role of Semantics and Pragmatics: In this section we point out shortcomings of the above approaches which consider only surface-level characteristics for generation. Through this we motivate the necessity of knowledge graphs and domain-specific ontologies to understand the concepts present in structured data and assist the generation step through a deeper understanding. In this section, we will present a unification of literature from knowledge graphs area, like entity resolution, relation canonicalization, *etc.*, KG embeddings as well as heuristics which encode domain-specific pragmatics coupled with NLG to infer and produce higher-level and more complex natural language discourse.

Open Problems and Future Directions: This part will focus on various aspects of natural language generation which are far from being realized. The presenters will get highly creative and also borrow connections from some recent trends (Jain et al., 2017; Munigala et al., 2018; Hu et al., 2017; Jain et al., 2019) in NLG literature to formulate future directions for automatic text generation. The goal of this section is not only to motivate and

[1]https://www.arria.com/

[2]https://automatedinsights.com/

convey open research problems, but mainly to start a discussion paving the way for newer problems in the area.

Conclusion and Closing Remarks: We close with discussions about all approaches and some practical (as well as funny) observations for practical NLG realizations.

5 URLs

Slides: https://drive.google.com/open?id=1HaGCNc6n_sjyGLdaGzAVPvAeT0ZhhL3Q
Website: https://sites.google.com/view/acl-19-nlg

6 Breadth

This tutorial has more than 60% material which are not research outputs of the presenters. Thus majority of the material covered is discussion of the work done by other researchers.

7 Prerequisite Knowledge

We would like to ensure that the tutorial is self-contained. We do not assume any specific expertise from the audience. However, general awareness about Natural Language Processing and Machine Learning, and Deep Learning methods (such as Recurrent Neural Network, and Sequence-to-Sequence models) will be helpful.

8 Presenter Details

Abhijit Mishra
(https://abhijitmishra.github.io)
is currently a part of IBM Research AI, Bangalore, India, serving as Research Scientist in the division of AI-Tech. He is involved in multiple projects based on Natural Language Generation (NLG), viz. (1) Controllable Text Transformation (2) Structured Data Summarization, and (3) Devising evaluation metrics for quality estimation of NLG Output. Prior to joining IBM Research, he was a Ph.D. student in the Department of Computer Science and Engineering, Indian Institute of Technology Bombay (graduated in 2017). Since 2013, Abhijit's works have been consistently getting published in the proceedings of prestigious NLP/AI conferences such as ACL, AAAI, and WWW. He has also given multiple talks in Cognitive NLP, and Natural Language Understanding and Generation. The full list of his publications and talks are available in his website.

Anirban Laha
(https://anirbanl.github.io/)
is currently associated with the AI Tech group at IBM Research AI - India. He is interested in applications of machine learning/deep learning in natural language processing. He has been working in natural language generation (NLG) project in IBM for the last two years and has published papers on abstractive summarization both from unstructured and structured data in top conferences like NeurIPS, ACL and NAACL. At IBM, he has also worked on argumentation mining (IBM Project Debater[3]), which received news coverage worldwide recently because of a live machine vs human debate[4]. He was also briefly associated with machine learning for creativity project at IBM (SIGKDD workshop[5]), during which he has worked on story generation. Before joining IBM, he had spent some time as Applied Scientist in Microsoft and SDE at Amazon.com. He had received his MS degree from Indian Institute of Science (IISc), Bangalore. He had given talks on NLG, particularly NLG from structured data in multiple venues. The full list of his publications and talks are available in his website.

Karthik Sankaranarayanan
(http://bit.do/gscholar-karthik)
is a Senior Research Scientist and Research Manager working in the area of Artificial Intelligence at IBM's India Research Lab in Bangalore. He is currently leading research projects focused around Natural Language Generation (NLG), question-answering (QA), multimodal deep learning, and information retrieval from domain-specific knowledge graphs (NLQ) as part of IBM Watson. He has also managed efforts around argumentation mining (IBM Project Debater[3]), which received news coverage worldwide recently because of a live machine vs human debate[4]. He has published in flagship AI and knowledge management conferences and journals such as NeurIPS, CVPR, AAAI, IJCAI, ACL, NAACL, Machine Learning Journal, KDD, SIGMOD, VLDB, among others. He is an active PC member at several top academic conferences in AI. His innovations have resulted in more than 30 patents around applications of AI to industry problems. He is a Senior Member of IEEE. Before joining IBM Research in 2011, he obtained

[3] http://bit.do/ibm-project-debater
[4] http://bit.do/theverge-debater
[5] https://ml4creativity.mybluemix.net/

his PhD in Computer Science from The Ohio State University. Recently, he was the lead organizer of "Machine Learning for Creativity" workshop[5] at SIGKDD 2017, held at Halifax, Canada which was co-organized by IBM, Google Brain, Sony CSL. This workshop was attended by around 50 researchers from academia as well as industry and featured keynote talks by faculty from Harvard, MIT, amongst other notable researchers.

Parag Jain
(`https://parajain.github.io/`)
is currently working as a Research Engineer in IBM India Research Lab. At IBM he has been working in natural language generation (NLG) and has published papers on summarization from tabular data in top NLP conference like NAACL-HLT. He has also briefly worked on ontology driven dialog systems focusing on template based natural language generation from structured outputs. Recently, he has also published on Unsupervised Controllable Text Formalization in AAAI 2019. Parag completed his Masters in Computer Science from IIT Hyderabad in 2015. His M.Tech thesis was titled "Metric Learning for Clustering in Streaming Large-Scale Data". Prior to joining IBM, he has worked at Amazon.com as an SDE for a year. His website has all details about his publications.

Saravanan Krishnan
(`http://bit.do/linkedin-saravanan`)
is currently associated with the AI Tech group at IBM Research AI India since 2014. He is interested in natural language processing generation, mono and cross lingual information retrieval, information extraction, data mining and applications of machine learning. He has been working in natural language generation (NLG) project in IBM for the last two years focusing on research-oriented solutions for industrial deployments. Earlier at IBM, he was part of information retrieval group in IBM Project Debater[3], which received news coverage worldwide recently because of a live machine vs human debate[4]. Before joining IBM, he was at Microsoft Research India as Software Development Engineer for 6 years and at Anna University, Chennai as Project Associate for five years. He has published many papers in conferences (LREC, CIKM, ECIR, EACL) and journals (AJIT, LNCS) in the past 15 years of his research career. His LinkedIn profile has more details.

References

Gabor Angeli, Percy Liang, and Dan Klein. 2010. A simple domain-independent probabilistic approach to generation. In *EMNLP*, EMNLP '10.

Dzmitry Bahdanau, Kyunghyun Cho, and Yoshua Bengio. 2014. Neural machine translation by jointly learning to align and translate. In *ICLR 2015*.

Satanjeev Banerjee and Alon Lavie. 2005. Meteor: An automatic metric for mt evaluation with improved correlation with human judgments. In *Proceedings of the ACL Workshop on Intrinsic and Extrinsic Evaluation Measures for Machine Translation and/or Summarization*, pages 65–72. Association for Computational Linguistics.

Junwei Bao, Duyu Tang, Nan Duan, Zhao Yan, Yuanhua Lv, Ming Zhou, and Tiejun Zhao. 2018. Table-to-text: Describing table region with natural language. *arXiv preprint arXiv:1805.11234*.

Regina Barzilay and Mirella Lapata. 2005. Collective content selection for concept-to-text generation. In *EMNLP*, HLT '05.

Anja Belz. 2008. Automatic generation of weather forecast texts using comprehensive probabilistic generation-space models. *Nat. Lang. Eng.*, 14(4):431–455.

Robert Dale, Sabine Geldof, and Jean-Philippe Prost. 2003. Coral : Using natural language generation for navigational assistance. In *Twenty-Sixth Australasian Computer Science Conference (ACSC2003)*, volume 16 of *CRPIT*, pages 35–44, Adelaide, Australia. ACS.

Dimitrios Galanis and Ion Androutsopoulos. 2007. Generating multilingual descriptions from linguistically annotated owl ontologies: The naturalowl system. In *ENLG*, ENLG '07.

Kavita Ganesan. 2018. Rouge 2.0: Updated and improved measures for evaluation of summarization tasks. *arXiv preprint arXiv:1803.01937*.

Claire Gardent, Anastasia Shimorina, Shashi Narayan, and Laura Perez-Beltrachini. 2017. Creating training corpora for micro-planners. In *ACL*.

Nancy Green. 2006. Generation of biomedical arguments for lay readers. In *Proceedings of the Fourth International Natural Language Generation Conference*, INLG '06, pages 114–121, Stroudsburg, PA, USA. Association for Computational Linguistics.

Zhiting Hu, Zichao Yang, Xiaodan Liang, Ruslan Salakhutdinov, and Eric P. Xing. 2017. Toward controlled generation of text. In *Proceedings of the 34th International Conference on Machine Learning*, volume 70 of *Proceedings of Machine Learning Research*, pages 1587–1596, International Convention Centre, Sydney, Australia. PMLR.

Parag Jain, Priyanka Agrawal, Abhijit Mishra, Mohak Sukhwani, Anirban Laha, and Karthik Sankaranarayanan. 2017. Story generation from sequence of independent short descriptions. *CoRR*, abs/1707.05501.

Parag Jain, Anirban Laha, Karthik Sankaranarayanan, Preksha Nema, Mitesh M. Khapra, and Shreyas Shetty. 2018. A mixed hierarchical attention based encoder-decoder approach for standard table summarization. In *NAACL-HLT*.

Parag Jain, Abhijit Mishra, Amar Prakash Azad, and Karthik Sankaranarayanan. 2019. Unsupervised controllable text formalization. In *AAAI*.

Joohyun Kim and Raymond J. Mooney. 2010. Generative alignment and semantic parsing for learning from ambiguous supervision. In *COLING*, COLING 10.

Ioannis Konstas and Mirella Lapata. 2012. Unsupervised concept-to-text generation with hypergraphs. In *NAACL-HLT*.

Irene Langkilde and Kevin Knight. 1998. Generation that exploits corpus-based statistical knowledge. In *ACL*, ACL '98, pages 704–710, Stroudsburg, PA, USA. Association for Computational Linguistics.

Rémi Lebret, David Grangier, and Michael Auli. 2016. Neural text generation from structured data with application to the biography domain. In *EMNLP*.

Franois Mairesse and Marilyn A. Walker. 2011. Controlling user perceptions of linguistic style: Trainable generation of personality traits. *Computational Linguistics*, 37(3):455–488.

Hongyuan Mei, Mohit Bansal, and Matthew R. Walter. 2016. What to talk about and how? selective generation using lstms with coarse-to-fine alignment. In *NAACL-HLT*.

Vitobha Munigala, Abhijit Mishra, Srikanth G. Tamilselvam, Shreya Khare, Riddhiman Dasgupta, and Anush Sankaran. 2018. Persuaide ! an adaptive persuasive text generation system for fashion domain. In *Companion of the The Web Conference 2018 on The Web Conference 2018, WWW 2018, Lyon , France, April 23-27, 2018*, pages 335–342.

Preksha Nema, Shreyas Shetty, Parag Jain, Anirban Laha, Karthik Sankaranarayanan, and Mitesh M. Khapra. 2018. Generating descriptions from structured data using a bifocal attention mechanism and gated orthogonalization. In *NAACL-HLT*.

Kishore Papineni, Salim Roukos, Todd Ward, and Wei-Jing Zhu. 2002. Bleu: a method for automatic evaluation of machine translation. In *ACL*, pages 311–318.

Ehud Reiter, Somayajulu Sripada, Jim Hunter, Jin Yu, and Ian Davy. 2005. Choosing words in computer-generated weather forecasts. *Artif. Intell.*, 167(1-2):137–169.

Radu Soricut and Daniel Marcu. 2006. Stochastic language generation using widl-expressions and its application in machine translation and summarization. In *ACL*, ACL-44, pages 1105–1112, Stroudsburg, PA, USA. Association for Computational Linguistics.

Ross Turner, Somayajulu Sripada, and Ehud Reiter. 2010. Generating approximate geographic descriptions. In *ENLG*, volume 5790.

Sam Wiseman, Stuart M Shieber, and Alexander M Rush. 2017. Challenges in data-to-document generation. *arXiv preprint arXiv:1707.08052*.

Sam Wiseman, Stuart M Shieber, and Alexander M Rush. 2018. Learning neural templates for text generation. *arXiv preprint arXiv:1808.10122*.

Wei Xu, Courtney Napoles, Ellie Pavlick, Quanze Chen, and Chris Callison-Burch. 2016. Optimizing statistical machine translation for text simplification. *Transactions of the Association for Computational Linguistics*, 4:401–415.

Author Index

Association for Computational Linguistics
209 N. Eighth Street
Stroudsburg, Pennsylvania 18360

ISBN 978-1-5108-9099-2

CURRAN ASSOCIATES INC.
proceedings.com